DISCIPLESHIP AND SPIRITUAL WARFARE

Discipleship *and* Spiritual Warfare

From the Screwtape Letters
to the Christian Life

THIAGO SILVA

WIPF & STOCK · Eugene, Oregon

DISCIPLESHIP AND SPIRITUAL WARFARE
From the Screwtape Letters to the Christian Life

Copyright © 2025 Thiago Silva. All rights reserved. Except for brief quotations in critical publications or reviews, no part of this book may be reproduced in any manner without prior written permission from the publisher. Write: Permissions, Wipf and Stock Publishers, 199 W. 8th Ave., Suite 3, Eugene, OR 97401.

Wipf & Stock
An Imprint of Wipf and Stock Publishers
199 W. 8th Ave., Suite 3
Eugene, OR 97401

www.wipfandstock.com

PAPERBACK ISBN: 979-8-3852-5373-9
HARDCOVER ISBN: 979-8-3852-5374-6
EBOOK ISBN: 979-8-3852-5375-3

"There is no neutral ground in the universe: every square inch, every split second, is claimed by God and counterclaimed by Satan."

— C. S. Lewis, *Christian Reflections.*

Table of contents

Preface ix

Chapter 1: Introduction 1

Chapter 2: Discipleship and Spiritual Warfare: A Biblical Vision 8

Chapter 3: The Banality of Temptation 18

Chapter 4: Distraction as a Weapon 28

Chapter 5: Affections and Formation 40

Chapter 6: Prayer and Resistance 49

Chapter 7: The Church as a Battleground 62

Chapter 8: Pain and Prosperity 73

Chapter 9: The Danger of Pride 85

Chapter 10: The Kingdom and the World 97

Chapter 11: The Christian Journey 109

Conclusion: Discipleship in the Fog of War 121

Bibliography 129

Preface

THE DEVIL DOES NOT come with horns and a pitchfork. He comes with half-truths, distractions, respectable sins, and a voice that sounds a little too much like our own. In *The Screwtape Letters*, C. S. Lewis (1898–1963) exposes this subtle warfare. He invites us behind enemy lines—not to frighten us with tales of demons, but to awaken us to the invisible war that rages every day in our hearts, habits, and affections. The world he builds is fiction, but the warfare it describes is not.

This book that you have in your hands, *Discipleship and Spiritual Warfare: From the Screwtape Letters to the Christian Life*, is not a commentary in the traditional sense. It does not decode Lewis's letters one by one or seek to press every metaphor into a theological mold. Instead, it is a theological and pastoral reflection on the world Lewis evokes—a world of spiritual battle and formation, where the Christian life is lived under enemy fire. It is a meditation on discipleship forged in the context of war.

Why this pairing—discipleship and spiritual warfare?

Because the Christian life is not a neutral journey of self-improvement. It is a war of allegiance. To follow Christ is to step into a contested space. It is to be claimed by grace and hunted by the enemy. It is to walk, daily, with Jesus through trials, temptations, sufferings, and small victories—learning how to pray, how to love, how to resist, how to persevere. And Lewis, through the inverted logic of his demons, teaches us how the enemy works so we might learn how grace prevails.

Preface

Lewis knew that war was not always dramatic. Often, it is dull. The weapons of hell are not always violence and chaos, but boredom, distraction, resentment, pride, spiritual apathy. *The Screwtape Letters* shows us how hell wages war not by overpowering believers, but by slowly numbing them—pulling them away from the truth one small compromise at a time. The patient does not fall with a crash, but with a drift. That insight, I believe, makes Lewis a great guide for discipleship in the modern era.

This book draws on Lewis's imaginative world to explore nine key dimensions of Christian formation—temptation, attention, affections, prayer, the church, suffering, perseverance, identity, and kingdom-mindedness. Each chapter reflects on a theme from *The Screwtape Letters*, connects it to Scripture and theology, and considers its practical significance for believers today. These reflections are deeply pastoral in intention: not abstract essays, but battle guides for Christians seeking to follow Jesus faithfully in a hostile world.

In writing this, I have had three audiences in mind:

First, I write for believers who have been captivated by Lewis's imagination and want to understand the theology underneath the fiction. You may have laughed at Screwtape's satire, flinched at its accuracy, or felt the sting of conviction. My hope is that this book will help you go deeper—into God's word, into theology, into your own heart.

Second, I write for pastors, teachers, and disciplers. Lewis's creative genius is a powerful tool in the hands of those who teach others. His stories open doors to hard doctrines. My prayer is that this book serves as a resource for your preaching, your small groups, and your conversations with those you mentor in the faith.

Third, I write for weary saints. For those who feel stuck in the fog. For those who wonder if they're still on the path. For those who have battled the same temptations for too long and feel no closer to holiness. I want to say this clearly: the enemy is real, but he is not sovereign. You are not alone. And you are not beyond the reach of God's grace. Spiritual warfare is not about the strength of your grip—it is about the grip of the One who holds you.

Preface

This book is not about demons. It is about Jesus. It is about grace that sustains. It is about a cross that has already conquered. And it is about the ordinary moments—when you say no to sin, when you show up to church tired, when you pray through dryness, when you love in obscurity—that God uses to shape his people.

Discipleship is spiritual warfare. But it is also grace upon grace. In the end, *The Screwtape Letters* is not a story of despair—it is a story that, through satire, points to victory. And so, too, I hope this book will do the same. Not by offering spiritual shortcuts or simple answers, but by calling you to that long obedience in the same direction. To resist the enemy. To follow Jesus. And to remember that the war has already been won on the cross.

May these reflections strengthen your walk, deepen your hope, sharpen your discernment, and stir your affection for Christ. He holds you fast.

Dr. Thiago Silva
Lake Charles, Louisiana

Chapter 1

Introduction

IN 1942, AMID THE thunder of falling bombs and the fractured silence of moral collapse across Europe, C. S. Lewis released a strange little book: a fictional collection of letters from a senior demon to his younger apprentice. *The Screwtape Letters* did not seem, at first, like a natural success. It was not inspirational. It was not doctrinal in the traditional sense. It offered no overt spiritual comfort. What it offered instead was a glimpse behind enemy lines—a dark mirror in which the Christian could see himself. And in that mirror, Lewis revealed what many had forgotten: that the Christian life is war, and the battlefield is the soul.

The brilliance of Lewis's vision lies not in grand revelations, but in everyday spiritual formation. The enemy's goal is not to lead the patient into dramatic sin, but to keep him spiritually asleep—bored with church, proud of his own humility, distracted by politics, enamored with shallow romance, skeptical of suffering, and indifferent to prayer. Screwtape aims not to destroy faith in a single blow, but to choke it through clutter. Every letter is a small lesson of how spiritual formation happens—not primarily in spectacular victories or defeats, but in a thousand daily choices of thought, habit, and heart.

That is why *The Screwtape Letters* remains enduringly relevant. Because discipleship—the real, lifelong process of being conformed to Christ—is shaped and tested in the ordinary. And because spiritual warfare is not reserved for the battlefield's edge; it unfolds in kitchens, classrooms, offices, and pews. Lewis knew this. He crafted a book that was not merely clever, but pastoral. Beneath the irony and satire is a fierce love for the soul and a deep concern for the church. The Christian life, as Lewis shows, is not an abstract idea or a weekend hobby. It is a long and dangerous journey toward glory, undertaken in enemy territory, where every day we are either drawing nearer to God or drifting away from him.

UNDERSTANDING THE SCREWTAPE LETTERS: CONTEXT AND CONTENT

When *The Screwtape Letters* was published in 1942, Britain was in the midst of World War II. The nation had endured the Blitz, lived under the constant threat of invasion, and was grappling with widespread suffering, fear, and loss. These conditions provoked deep moral and spiritual questions in the hearts of many. Into this context, C. S. Lewis offered a satirical and imaginative reflection on the nature of temptation and the subtle workings of evil in everyday life. Originally published as a weekly serial in *The Guardian* (an Anglican religious newspaper) in 1941, the letters portrayed the Christian life not in dramatic heroics, but in the mundane and ordinary—precisely where most spiritual battles are won or lost.

At the time, Lewis was gaining a national audience through his BBC radio talks, which would later be compiled into *Mere Christianity*. His voice resonated in a culture increasingly marked by secularism, skepticism, and the waning influence of traditional Christianity. *The Screwtape Letters* confronted these shifts with wit and theological insight, using the fictional correspondence of a senior demon to reveal how distraction, pride, and spiritual apathy thrive under the guise of normal life. Lewis's blend of satire, theology, and imaginative apologetics offered both cultural critique and spiritual counsel for an anxious and war-weary generation.

The book consists of 31 fictional letters from Screwtape, a senior demon, to his inexperienced nephew Wormwood, a junior

INTRODUCTION

tempter assigned to a newly converted Christian referred to simply as "the patient." Through Screwtape's cynical and condescending voice, we receive a profoundly insightful (and often painfully accurate) depiction of the tactics used by spiritual forces to derail Christian faith and formation. Each letter unpacks a particular theme or temptation: pride, distraction, relationships, spiritual dryness, suffering, and even the misuse of church and politics. There are no chapters in the traditional sense—only letters, each building on the last, as Wormwood's efforts to corrupt his patient continue with increasing urgency.

What makes the book so powerful is Lewis's use of inverted theology. Screwtape refers to God as "the Enemy" and describes Christian virtues like humility, chastity, and love with disgust. This reverse perspective forces the reader to think theologically from the underside. We are invited to observe the Christian life not through idealism, but through the lens of spiritual opposition. And in doing so, we begin to recognize the subtlety of temptation—not merely in evil acts, but in distorted desires, habits, and loves.

Screwtape warns Wormwood not to rely on dramatic sins. He encourages small, slow erosion: encouraging the patient to critique sermons more than apply them; to pray with vague emotion rather than honest confession; to fixate on the faults of fellow church members; to idolize comfort and security; to spiritualize political commitments while forgetting the gospel. As such, *The Screwtape Letters* is not a handbook on demonic activity—it's a mirror reflecting the fragile journey of discipleship in a fallen world.

Theologically, the book is saturated with Lewis's understanding of sanctification. Though he was not writing a systematic theology, Lewis's vision is biblical: the Christian life is a process of being conformed to Christ through the ordinary and the difficult, through suffering, community, repentance, and obedience. Screwtape's fury rises when the patient grows spiritually without feeling anything, when he resists temptation quietly, or when he prays sincerely even in doubt. For Lewis, these are the marks of true discipleship.

Moreover, the book ends not with a spectacular display of spiritual victory, but with death—the moment Screwtape calls "the Enemy's territory." And yet it is here that the patient finds peace. He is received into glory, not because of his strength, but because he was kept. He persevered, haltingly but truly, and the devils lost their grip.

This is what makes the *Screwtape Letters* such a compelling book for modern discipleship. It is not a fantasy. It is realism cloaked in fiction. It names what we often ignore: that every Christian is in a battle, not just against external pressures, but internal drift. That our minds and hearts are constantly being formed—and that intentional, grace-shaped discipleship is the only true resistance.

A PORTRAIT OF THE DISCIPLE IN PROCESS

The patient, the anonymous man at the heart of the *Screwtape Letters*, is not a spiritual hero. He is not a martyr, mystic, or visionary. He is not a saint whose life will one day be inscribed in stained glass. He is, by all appearances, unremarkable. And that is precisely what makes him powerful. Because he is us.

Lewis chose not to give the patient a name, not to render him extraordinary, but to present him as an everyman—a composite of countless believers stumbling forward in the Christian life. He is converted early in the story, begins attending church, prays (though inconsistently), and tries to live a moral life. But he is often confused. He struggles with lust, pride, fear, laziness, and spiritual dryness. His affections are mixed. His motives are unclear. His convictions are under pressure. He is influenced by culture, friendships, intellectual fads, and personal pain. And yet, through all of this, something real is taking shape in him. He is being discipled—not in a programmatic or institutional sense, but in the formative spiritual sense. His life is being shaped—either conformed to Christ, or deformed by the world.

Screwtape's instructions provide a sinister curriculum of anti-discipleship. His aim is not to destroy the patient in one fell swoop,

INTRODUCTION

but to keep him from ever growing. He trains Wormwood to encourage complacency, to exploit emotion, to nurture passivity. He distorts the patient's view of prayer by making it self-focused. He corrupts humility by making the patient proud of being humble. He even turns the church into a source of irritation—amplifying the hypocrisy of others, magnifying social differences, and dulling spiritual vitality through routine.

And yet, what frustrates Screwtape most is that the patient begins to change—not dramatically, but genuinely. He begins to obey even when it doesn't feel good. He repents without self-justification. He turns to God even in the absence of spiritual comfort. These are the moments when Screwtape's grip weakens. For in these quiet acts of obedience, the patient is maturing. He is being sanctified—not in glory, but in grit.

His perseverance is not impressive by worldly standards. It is not dramatic. It is not even very visible. It is fragile. But it is real. He keeps praying. He keeps going to church. He keeps confessing. He keeps walking. And by the end of the letters, when death arrives, it is not terror but triumph. He is welcomed into the presence of Christ—not because he achieved greatness, but because grace held him fast. He does not enter as a spiritual celebrity, but as a disciple. And that is enough.

This is what makes *The Screwtape Letters* so powerful, especially today. It does not present the Christian life in airbrushed, heroic tones. It paints in gray, in struggle, in quiet faith. It acknowledges doubt, temptation, exhaustion, and sin—and still insists that God is at work in the midst of it all. It reminds us that discipleship is not reserved for the strong. It is for the weak who cling to grace. It is for the anxious who return to Christ. It is for the tired who do not give up. In other words, it is for us.

The patient's story is not one of spiritual excellence. It is one of faithfulness. And in the end, that is what sanctification looks like: slow, costly, ordinary, and beautiful. The story of the patient assures us that discipleship is possible—not just for the exceptional, but for everyone who says, "Lord, I believe—help my unbelief."

Discipleship and Spiritual Warfare

WHAT THIS BOOK OFFERS

This is not a commentary on *The Screwtape Letters*. It is not a literary analysis of Lewis's language, structure, or style. Nor is it an attempt to decode every line or trace a precise theology from his fiction. Rather, this book is a theological meditation and pastoral reflection on the spiritual world Lewis evokes—a world that, while imagined, uncovers deep truths about the ordinary battles of the Christian life.

The Screwtape Letters was never meant to entertain, but to expose. Behind the satire lies a sobering vision of the soul's formation in a world charged with temptation, distortion, and unseen opposition. What Lewis offers is not demonology, but discipleship—in reverse. By showing how a demon thinks, he reveals how a Christian grows. This book seeks to walk alongside Lewis's insights and place them in conversation with Scripture, theology, and the lived reality of Christian formation.

The structure of this book mirrors the journey of Christian formation. It begins with a foundation: in Chapter 2, "Discipleship and Spiritual Warfare: A Biblical Vision," we explore the biblical theology of spiritual warfare and discipleship. This sets the stage for all that follows, rooting our reflections in the truth that to follow Christ is to engage in a lifelong spiritual battle.

From there, each chapter unpacks a theme central to the believer's growth and the enemy's strategies based on Lewis's work. In Chapter 3, "The Banality of Temptation," we see how hell prefers not dramatic rebellion, but slow spiritual drift—compromise masked as normalcy. Chapter 4, "Distraction as a Weapon," uncovers how noise, hurry, and triviality wear down our attention and affections for God. Chapter 5, "Affections and Formation," reminds us that we are shaped not only by what we think but by what we love—and how easily our loves are deformed.

Chapter 6, "Prayer and Resistance," draws us into the war zone of prayer—where the enemy distracts, discourages, and distorts, yet where grace draws us near to God again and again. In Chapter 7, "The Church as a Battleground," we confront the way the enemy

INTRODUCTION

weaponizes our frustrations with community, even while God uses that same community to sanctify and strengthen us. Chapter 8, "Pain and Prosperity," explores the dangers of prosperity and how hardship, rather than destroying faith, often becomes the very soil in which perseverance grows.

Chapter 9, "The Danger of Pride," examines how even our virtues can become vices when twisted by self-focus. Chapter 10, "The Kingdom and the World," takes up the cultural battlefield—how the enemy tempts us to replace Kingdom-centered discipleship with politicized religion or vague spirituality. Finally, in Chapter 11, "The Christian Journey," we trace the spiritual arc of Lewis's unnamed protagonist—flawed, inconsistent, but ultimately preserved by grace. His story is ours: not triumphant in appearance, but victorious in Christ.

After these explorations, the Conclusion, *"Discipleship in the Fog of War,"* draws the threads together into a pastoral exhortation: that to walk with Christ is to walk into battle—but never alone. The war is real, the stakes are eternal, and the grace of God is sufficient.

Taken together, these chapters form a discipleship guide for our time. They are written for the weary and the watchful—for those who are just beginning their walk with Christ and for those who have been bruised by battle. They are for pastors, mentors, small groups, parents, students, and saints who long to be formed in truth and fortified in grace.

Above all, they are for the church. For the church is not the backdrop to this story—it is the battleground, the training ground, and the testimony that Screwtape has not had the final word. The gates of hell will not prevail against the church, because the risen Christ reigns, and he is building his people, one persevering disciple at a time.

This book is not about defeating the devil with clever insight. It is about enduring in Christ through slow, honest, grace-dependent formation. In that formation, the battle is already being won.

Chapter 2

Discipleship and Spiritual Warfare: A Biblical Vision

WHEN JESUS CALLED HIS first disciples, he did not offer them a life of comfort, convenience, or cultural acceptance. He offered them a cross. "Follow me," he said, "and I will make you fishers of men" (Matt 4:19). "If anyone would come after me, let him deny himself and take up his cross daily and follow me" (Luke 9:23). "In the world you will have tribulation. But take heart; I have overcome the world" (John 16:33).

From the very beginning, the Christian life was presented not as a path of ease, but as a journey of costly allegiance. To be a disciple of Christ is to live in the middle of a battlefield—between the kingdom of God and the kingdom of darkness, between the new life in the Spirit and the old ways of the flesh, between the promises of God and the lies of the enemy.

In every age, discipleship and spiritual warfare have been inseparable. They are not two different aspects of the Christian life—they are the same reality viewed from two perspectives. Discipleship is the positive pursuit of becoming like Christ. Spiritual warfare is the inevitable conflict that arises as we seek to do so. And the Bible makes this vision unmistakably clear.

Discipleship and Spiritual Warfare: A Biblical Vision

THE REALITY OF SPIRITUAL WARFARE

From beginning to end, Scripture presents a world charged with conflict. This is not simply the clash of civilizations or political ideologies, but a deeper, older, and more invisible war—a spiritual war. It is a battle not over territory, but over truth. Not over land, but over souls.

The biblical worldview is unapologetically supernatural. It does not reduce human struggle to social structures or psychological patterns, though it affirms the importance of both. Rather, it reveals a reality in which every human being lives in the midst of a cosmic conflict between the kingdom of God and the forces of darkness.

This warfare begins in Eden. Genesis 3 is not only the account of humanity's fall—it is the first recorded act of spiritual deception. Satan, appearing as a serpent, slithers into the garden not with a sword, but with a question: "Did God actually say...?" (Gen 3:1). The first attack is not against Adam and Eve's bodies, but against their trust in the character and goodness of God. The serpent redefines sin as freedom and reimagines obedience as oppression. The first spiritual battle is a battle of theology—and the effects are catastrophic.

From there, the enemy continues his work. In Job 1–2, Satan appears as the accuser of the righteous, challenging the integrity of faith and seeking permission to afflict God's servant. In Zechariah 3, he stands at the right hand of the high priest, hurling accusations. In 1 Chronicles 21, he tempts David to sin by numbering Israel. Satan is never idle. His strategy is multidimensional—he deceives, tempts, accuses, and divides. He aims to destroy the people of God not by storming their gates, but by slowly undermining their allegiance, their love, and their discernment.

The gospels of Matthew, Mark, Luke, and John heighten the urgency of this conflict. Jesus does not enter a spiritually neutral world. He comes into occupied territory. In Matthew 4, the devil tempts him in the wilderness with distortions of Scripture and offers of glory without suffering. Christ's victory in that moment foreshadows his ultimate triumph at the cross. Yet the battle continues through his ministry, as he casts out demons, confronts false religion, and teaches his disciples to pray, "Deliver us from the evil one."

The apostolic writings assume this warfare as normative. Paul tells the Ephesians that "we do not wrestle against flesh and blood," but against spiritual powers that stand opposed to God and his purposes (Eph 6:12). Peter warns that our adversary the devil "prowls around like a roaring lion" (1 Pet 5:8), and James commands believers to "resist the devil, and he will flee from you" (James 4:7). These are not rhetorical flourishes. They are urgent calls to remain watchful, grounded in truth, and rooted in Christ.

Yet the Scriptures do not leave us with a dualistic vision of an evenly matched battle. Christ has already won the decisive victory. On the cross, he "disarmed the rulers and authorities and put them to open shame" (Col 2:15). His resurrection shattered the reign of death, sin, and Satan. The devil is a defeated foe—still dangerous, but bound. Still active, but doomed. The war continues, but the end is not in doubt.

Therefore, spiritual warfare is not peripheral to the Christian life—it is the context in which it unfolds. From the fall to the final return of Christ, the battle is real. But so is the triumph of grace.

DISCIPLESHIP AS SPIRITUAL WARFARE

If spiritual warfare is the context of the Christian life, then discipleship is the strategy of resistance. The two are not separate realities but two perspectives on the same calling. Discipleship is the long obedience of becoming like Christ; spiritual warfare is the battle that inevitably arises as we pursue that goal in a world opposed to it. To follow Jesus is to enter a conflict. It is to defect from the dominion of darkness and pledge allegiance to a crucified King. It is to live in enemy territory with the banner of a greater kingdom over your head.

Jesus never hid this reality from his disciples. His invitation—"Follow me"—was also a summons to die. "If anyone would come

Discipleship and Spiritual Warfare: A Biblical Vision

after me, let him deny himself and take up his cross and follow me" (Matt 16:24). This is not sentimental spirituality. It is self-denial, spiritual resistance, and costly allegiance. Every act of obedience, every step of repentance, every surrender of pride and preference is an act of war against the enemy who desires our soul. Every time a believer says no to sin, yes to truth, yes to Christ—hell loses ground.

This is why the enemy opposes true discipleship with such ferocity. Satan is not primarily concerned with making people wicked. He is content to keep them distracted, comfortable, apathetic, and unformed. A Christian who professes faith but remains spiritually stagnant poses little threat. But a Christian being conformed to the image of Christ, who is learning to forgive, to pray, to serve, to worship, to love, to suffer faithfully—that disciple is a danger to the gates of hell. The enemy resists sanctification because it declares that Christ's reign is real and advancing.

This is why Paul describes the Christian life in combative terms. "Fight the good fight of the faith" (1 Tim 6:12). "Put to death what is earthly in you" (Col 3:5). "Put on the Lord Jesus Christ, and make no provision for the flesh" (Rom 13:14). These are not the words of passive spirituality. They are the language of war. Discipleship involves conflict—not only with the world around us, but with the sin within us.

And yet this warfare is not waged in our own strength. The disciple of Jesus is not left to fight alone. Christ has gone before us and broken the power of sin. The Spirit dwells within us, enabling what the flesh cannot accomplish. God's word instructs and sustains us. The church walks with us, encouraging and correcting as we grow. We are called to battle, but we are not conscripts—we are sons and daughters of the King, already accepted, already loved, already victorious in him.

True discipleship, then, is not merely information transfer or behavioral improvement. It is the Spirit-empowered, grace-driven, Scripture-saturated formation of a soul in resistance to the devil's schemes and submission to Christ's lordship. It is warfare in slow motion. Not spectacular, but steady. Not showy, but faithful.

Discipleship and Spiritual Warfare

In a world shaped by sin, and an age ruled by distraction, discipleship is not safe. But it is the only path that leads to life. And it is the way Jesus walks with us—step by step, through every skirmish, toward glory.

THE WEAPONS OF OUR WARFARE

To be engaged in spiritual warfare is not simply to endure conflict—it is to be equipped for it. Scripture does not call the Christian to survive on instinct or willpower, but to stand firm in the strength and armor of God. In Ephesians 6, Paul draws back the curtain and gives the church its combat manual: not a new strategy, but ancient weapons—divinely given, spiritually empowered, and entirely sufficient.

"Finally," Paul writes, "be strong in the Lord and in the strength of his might" (Eph 6:10). The opening command is not, "Be strong," but "Be strong in the Lord." The foundation of spiritual warfare is not our strength but God's. Any attempt to resist temptation or pursue holiness apart from his power is doomed from the start. Victory in the Christian life is not about gritting our teeth; it is about resting in the triumph of Christ and standing with the armor he provides.

Paul goes on: "Put on the whole armor of God, that you may be able to stand against the schemes of the devil" (Eph 6:11). The enemy is not random or reactionary. He is strategic, and his methods are many—deception, accusation, distraction, discouragement. God's people are not left unarmed. But neither are they automatically protected. The command to "put on" the armor implies intentionality. Discipleship involves learning to dress for battle.

The armor includes six pieces, each vital for our defense and endurance. First, the belt of truth—wrapped around the core of our being, grounding us in the objective reality of God's Word in a world of lies. Second, the breastplate of righteousness—not our own moral effort, but the righteousness of Christ imputed to us and lived out in grateful obedience, protecting the heart from condemnation. Third, the shoes of the readiness given by the gospel of peace—stability, mobility, and courage rooted in the good news that we are reconciled to God and sent into the world.

Fourth, Paul tells us to take up the shield of faith, with which we can extinguish "all the flaming darts of the evil one" (Eph 6:16)—those sudden lies, haunting doubts, intrusive temptations that seek to pierce and overwhelm. Faith is not mere optimism; it is the settled trust in the character of God, based on the promises of God. Fifth, the helmet of salvation, guarding the mind—reminding the disciple that our identity is secure, our future is fixed, and our Savior is faithful.

And finally, the sword of the Spirit, which is the word of God—our only offensive weapon. This is no blunt instrument of human argument or speculation, but the living and active word of God, able to cut through confusion, expose sin, and defeat the enemy, as Jesus himself demonstrated in the wilderness (Matt 4). We fight by wielding what is written.

But Paul adds one more essential: "praying at all times in the Spirit" (Eph 6:18). Prayer is not a passive posture—it is active warfare. It is the constant communication of the soldier with the Commander. It is the breath of the battle-worn disciple, the lifeline to divine strength, the means by which we call in aid and intercede for others.

These weapons are not flashy. They will not trend. They will not entertain. But they are enough. For in Christ, the armor fits. And in the Spirit, they work. To be a disciple in a world at war is to learn how to wear the armor daily—not as costume, but as necessity. The battle is real. But so is the armor. And so is the victory.

THE BATTLE FOR THE MIND AND THE HEART

Spiritual warfare is not only fought in the realm of action. It is waged in the realm of attention, affection, imagination, and desire. Long before a Christian stumbles into visible sin, long before obedience is neglected in the open, there is often a subtle erosion within the inner life. The battlefield of discipleship runs through the mind and the heart. It is here that the enemy does some of his most dangerous work—not with direct confrontation, but with redirection; not through blasphemy, but through distraction.

Scripture repeatedly emphasizes the centrality of the mind in the Christian life. "Do not be conformed to this world," Paul writes, "but be transformed by the renewal of your mind" (Rom 12:2). Transformation does not begin in the hands or habits, but in the thoughts and patterns of belief that shape how we see God, ourselves, and the world. In 2 Corinthians 10:5, Paul declares that the weapons of our warfare are powerful "to destroy strongholds," and what are these strongholds? "Arguments and every lofty opinion raised against the knowledge of God," and we are called to "take every thought captive to obey Christ."

This is more than intellectual discipline. It is a spiritual act. To bring every thought into submission to Christ is to resist the enemy's long-standing strategy of twisting truth, planting doubt, and confusing what is good, beautiful, and holy. The enemy rarely storms the gates with an obvious lie. He works more often through slight distortions—half-truths that appeal to our pride or fear. His goal is to shape our minds with assumptions and narratives that slowly pull us away from the voice of our Shepherd.

But the heart is also under siege. In Scripture, the heart is not merely the seat of emotion; it is the center of desire and direction. Proverbs 4:23 urges, "Keep your heart with all vigilance, for from it flow the springs of life." The heart is where our loves are ordered—or disordered. It is where our worship is rooted. And this is why spiritual formation is ultimately a matter of spiritual warfare: because every day, we are being formed to love either the world or the Lord.

This is the genius of the enemy's strategy in our modern age. He does not need to argue people out of the faith. He simply needs to fill their minds with triviality and fill their hearts with lesser loves. He uses busyness to keep us from reflection. He uses pleasure to numb us from conviction. He uses comparison to distort our contentment. He does not have to make us atheists—just

DISCIPLESHIP AND SPIRITUAL WARFARE: A BIBLICAL VISION

distracted consumers. If he can shape our habits, he can shape our loves. And if he shapes our loves, he shapes our lives.

But the gospel is stronger. Christ not only claims our salvation—he reorders our affections. He not only commands our obedience—he renews our minds. The word of God is our standard. The Spirit of God is our strength. And the people of God are our community. Through these means, discipleship becomes a long process of resisting lies, loving truth, and slowly learning to desire what God desires.

To win the battle for the mind and the heart is not to escape the world, but to see the world rightly—through the lens of the gospel. To love what is eternal. To think with Scripture. To feel with compassion. To believe with clarity. This is how the disciple wages war. Not loudly, but faithfully. Not perfectly, but persistently.

PREPARING FOR THE LONG WAR

One of the most neglected truths about the Christian life is that it is long. While conversion may happen in a moment, transformation takes a lifetime.1 Discipleship is not an event—it is a journey. And in a culture of quick fixes, instant results, and spiritual shortcuts, the church must recover the biblical vision of faithfulness that

---

1. Conversion, or regeneration, is the sovereign act of God by which he imparts spiritual life to the sinner, bringing them out of spiritual death and into union with Christ (John 3:3-8; Titus 3:5; Eph 2:4-5). This moment of new birth is instantaneous and irreversible, marking the beginning of the Christian life. However, sanctification—our transformation into Christlikeness—is a lifelong process that follows conversion (Rom 12:2; 2 Cor 3:18; Phil 2:12-13). It involves the believer's active cooperation with the Holy Spirit in putting off the old self and growing in holiness (Col 3:5-10). As John Calvin writes, "The whole of our salvation and every part of it are comprehended in Christ," but this salvation unfolds in stages, with sanctification being a continual progress of dying to ourselves and being renewed to the image of God (Calvin, *Institutes*, 2.16.19; 3.3.9). It is within this process of sanctification that the believer engages in daily spiritual warfare—against the flesh, the world, and the devil (Eph 6:10-18; Gal 5:17). Thus, while conversion may happen in a moment, the transformation of the whole person is the ongoing battleground of discipleship.

endures. To follow Jesus is not to fight a single battle, but to enlist in a lifelong campaign. It is not a sprint—it is a marathon of war.

The apostle Paul understood this well. As he neared the end of his ministry, reflecting on decades of hardship, labor, and perseverance, he wrote: "I have fought the good fight, I have finished the race, I have kept the faith" (2 Tim 4:7). Those are not the words of someone who coasted to the end. They are the words of a weathered soldier—battered, scarred, and yet steadfast. He did not say, "I won every battle," but "I kept the faith." This is what it means to prepare for the long war: to know that your greatest spiritual triumph is not in how high you soared, but in how faithfully you endured.

Preparation for a long war requires realistic expectations. New believers, especially, must be taught that the Christian life is not free of pain, temptation, doubt, or spiritual struggle. In fact, conversion intensifies the conflict. When you become a Christian, you do not escape the enemy's attention—you attract it. You have been rescued from the dominion of darkness and brought into the kingdom of Christ (Col 1:13), and the devil does not take that loss quietly.

But we are not sent into the war unequipped. God supplies what is needed, not only in the moment of crisis, but in the daily rhythms of grace. What prepares a Christian to endure is not dramatic spiritual experiences, but a deep life of prayer, a regular diet of Scripture, weekly worship with the church, humble repentance, and spiritual friendships that speak truth in love.

The church plays a crucial role here. We are not individual soldiers fighting alone in the field—we are part of a battalion. The local church is not simply a place of teaching or encouragement; it is the spiritual training ground where disciples are prepared for endurance. In the gathered body, we learn to bear burdens, confront sin, serve one another, rejoice together, and stand firm side by side. A disciple without a church is like a soldier without an army—isolated, vulnerable, and exposed.

To prepare for the long war also means to learn the art of recovering. Even the most faithful Christian will grow tired. Some battles will be lost. Some seasons will feel dark and dry. But this is why God gives his people the promise of perseverance. Not that we will never fail—but that he will never fail us. "He who began a good work in you will bring it to completion at the day of Jesus Christ" (Phil 1:6).

To live as a disciple in a fallen world is to live with scars and stories, trials and triumphs. But it is also to walk with Christ, who knows our weakness, who sustains our steps, and who promises to finish what he started. Prepare to walk slowly. Prepare to suffer well. Prepare to endure with hope. The war is long, but the King is faithful.

Chapter 3

The Banality of Temptation

"Indeed the safest road to Hell is the gradual one—the gentle slope, soft underfoot, without sudden turnings, without milestones, without signposts." — *Screwtape*, Letter 12.

WHEN WE THINK OF spiritual warfare, we often envision something loud—chaotic, aggressive, apocalyptic. We picture temptation as a sudden crisis, a dramatic fork in the road between righteousness and ruin. We imagine Satan coming with fangs bared, wielding temptation like a club. But this is not usually how the enemy works. If the devil had his way, spiritual warfare wouldn't look like war at all. It would feel familiar, harmless, comfortable, and even religious.

This is what Lewis captures with piercing clarity in Letter 12. In this letter, the senior demon Screwtape tells his protégé Wormwood not to focus on "spectacular wickedness." He warns that the goal is not dramatic sin but gradual erosion. Not rebellion, but drift. As Screwtape writes, "It does not matter how small the sins are, provided that their cumulative effect is to edge the man away from the Light and out into the Nothing." The safest road to destruction, he insists, is the one that doesn't feel dangerous at all.

This is the first great lesson of discipleship in spiritual warfare: sin does not always begin as something monstrous. It begins in the mundane. It begins with forgetfulness. It begins when the disciple slowly stops paying attention. And it's precisely that subtlety that makes temptation so deadly.

THE BANALITY OF EVIL

The phrase "banality of evil" is often associated with political theorist Hannah Arendt, who used it to describe the shocking ordinariness of Adolf Eichmann, the Nazi bureaucrat responsible for managing the logistics of the Holocaust.[1] Arendt was struck not by Eichmann's monstrous personality, but by his boring efficiency. Evil, she suggested, is not always carried out by fanatics. Sometimes it's carried out by functionaries—people who simply follow the easiest path without reflection.

Lewis's vision of temptation is similar. The road to destruction, as Screwtape makes clear, is paved not with acts of grand rebellion, but with quiet compromises and the avoidance of God. It's not about doing terrible things. It's about doing nothing.

Screwtape describes his satisfaction that the "patient" is slipping away from faith not because of scandal or heresy, but because of "nothing." As he writes: "You will say that these are very small sins; and doubtless, like all young tempters, you are anxious to be able to report spectacular wickedness. But do remember, the only thing that matters is the extent to which you separate the man from the Enemy [God]" (Letter 12). In other words, Screwtape isn't after drama. He's after drift. This is spiritual entropy—the soul's quiet decline into lukewarmness. The genius of temptation is not its boldness, but its boredom.

Jesus warned of this very danger. In the parable of the soils (Matt 13:1–23), some seed falls among thorns—those who receive the word but are choked by "the cares of the world and the

---

1. The phrase "the banality of evil" appears in the subtitle of Arendt's book and is further developed in her reflections on Adolf Eichmann's trial. She argues that Eichmann was not a fanatical ideologue, but disturbingly ordinary — a man who failed to think critically about his actions, revealing evil as banal, bureaucratic, and thoughtless. See Hannah Arendt, *Eichmann in Jerusalem: A Report on the Banality of Evil* (1963).

deceitfulness of riches." What kills their spiritual growth? Not persecution or hatred of God, but distraction. Satan doesn't need to turn you into an atheist. He just needs to keep you scrolling.

Theologically, this reveals a crucial insight about sin: it is not only an act but also a trajectory. According to the Bible, sin is not just something we *do*—it is something that distorts who we *are*, and where we are *headed*. Sanctification and apostasy are rarely instantaneous. They unfold over time, through the shaping of our habits, desires, and choices.

John Owen, the great Puritan theologian, wrote, "Sin always aims at the utmost; every time it rises up to tempt or entice, might it have its own course, it would go out to the utmost sin in that kind."[2] What Owen means is that no sin is static. Every sinful habit wants to grow. It never stays where it is. And that's what makes small sins dangerous. They are seeds.

This is precisely Screwtape's strategy. He doesn't begin with blasphemy or apostasy. He begins with fatigue, with putting off prayer, with a little more self-pity, a little more preoccupation with how others see us. These are the "little foxes that spoil the vineyard" (Song of Songs 2:15). They are barely noticed—until it's too late.

Lewis writes elsewhere that "every time you make a choice you are turning the central part of you, the part of you that chooses... into something a little different than it was before."[3] The moral and spiritual self is constantly in motion—toward God or away. There is no such thing as neutral spiritual ground.

ORDINARY LIFE AS SPIRITUAL BATTLEGROUND

One of the central messages of the *Screwtape Letters* is that ordinary life is not spiritually neutral. For the Christian, there is no such thing as "just a day." Every conversation, every decision, every moment of prayer (or distraction from it) is part of the larger

---

2. Owen, *The Mortification of Sin*, 54.
3. Lewis, *Mere Christianity* III.4.

THE BANALITY OF TEMPTATION

spiritual conflict between the kingdom of God and the kingdom of darkness. As Screwtape says in Letter 1, the goal is not to argue a man out of Christianity, but simply to make sure he forgets it in the bustle of daily life. When a spiritual thought arises, just "suggest it's time for lunch."

This may seem almost comic, but it is devastatingly true. How many deep spiritual insights, how many moments of repentance or praise, have been aborted because of a text message, a craving, a phone call, or a mental rabbit trail? As Screwtape tells Wormwood in Letter 12: "You can make him do nothing at all for long periods. You can keep him up late at night, not roistering, but staring at a dead fire in a cold room." Lewis is challenging a common misconception—that the devil primarily works by adding things (evil thoughts, temptations, heresies). In fact, his best work is often by subtraction—keeping the Christian from truth, from prayer, from Scripture, from presence. His goal is emptiness.

The apostle Paul warned the Corinthian church to be aware of Satan's schemes (2 Cor 2:11). One of those schemes is to turn the ordinary into a trap. Work becomes distraction. Rest becomes laziness. Conversation becomes gossip. Even churchgoing becomes an exercise in self-righteousness or judgmentalism. Screwtape doesn't care what you're doing, as long as you're not doing it with God.

THE LOSS OF MILESTONES AND SIGNPOSTS

The most chilling line in Letter 12 may be this: "The safest road to Hell is the gradual one—the gentle slope, soft underfoot, without sudden turnings, without milestones, without signposts." Here Lewis summarizes the deceptive smoothness of spiritual decay. In the absence of crises, we assume all is well. We measure our souls by comfort, not by communion. But the absence of pain is not the presence of God.

Lewis is warning against one of the devil's most subtle and effective tools: spiritual drift. Unlike blatant rebellion or visible moral collapse, drift is quiet, slow, and often imperceptible. It happens not through denial of the faith, but through neglect. The soul does not fall off a cliff; it slowly drifts out to sea. One day of prayerlessness becomes a week, then a month. Scripture becomes less nourishing, worship less urgent, fellowship less vital. The enemy need not stir up scandal or crisis—he only needs to lull the believer into distraction, comfort, and forgetfulness. Lewis understood that hell's strategy is often more about dullness than destruction, more about inattention than assault.

This is precisely the warning we hear in Hebrews: "We must pay much closer attention to what we have heard, lest we drift away from it" (Heb 2:1). The danger is not always that we will storm out of the kingdom in defiance, but that we will slowly drift from it in complacency. The greatest threats are often not sudden explosions of sin but slow erosions of faith. Drift occurs when we stop anchoring ourselves to Christ through word, prayer, and community. The tide of the world is always pulling us, and if we are not actively resisting, we are already moving away.

This is where the modern world makes temptation even easier. Most of us are drowning in a sea of triviality. Our days are filled with small decisions that pull our gaze downward. And because nothing seems sinful, we don't recognize it as dangerous. Lewis saw this coming. Screwtape's method is perfectly suited to an age of screens, noise, and shallow pleasures.

HOPE: THE GRACE THAT INTERRUPTS THE DRIFT

Yet the *Screwtape Letters* is not a despairing book. Its brilliance lies in revealing temptation's subtlety—but its hope lies in reminding us that grace is more subtle still.

For every tactic of the enemy, God provides a deeper, sturdier counterforce. What Screwtape dreads most is when a Christian, even in spiritual dryness, continues to pray, continues to obey, continues to seek God without consolation. That's where real victory lies. As he writes in Letter 8: "Do not be deceived, Wormwood. Our cause is never more in danger than when a human… still intends to do our Enemy's will and looks round upon a universe from which every trace of Him seems to have vanished, and asks why he has been forsaken, and still obeys."

That, Lewis suggests, is true discipleship. It is not easy. It is not always joyful. It is often dry, quiet, and ordinary. But it is real. And it is effective. Satan cannot stop obedience. He can only distract from it.

PASTORAL-THEOLOGICAL REFLECTION

If Screwtape had his way, the soul would never be shocked into awareness. It would never face a crisis loud enough to awaken repentance, nor a joy deep enough to awaken desire. The goal would be neither heresy nor scandal. The goal would be numbness. And it is achieved not with a shout but with a whisper. The safest road to hell, Lewis warns us through Screwtape, is the gentle slope—soft underfoot, without sudden turnings, without milestones, without signposts. This is the strategy of *acedia*.[4]

Acedia, according to the ancient church, is a kind of spiritual listlessness, a sorrow in the face of spiritual good, a deep-seated boredom with God. We might call it sloth, but that word is often misunderstood. Sloth is not simply laziness. It is not doing nothing. It is doing everything except the one thing needful. It is not refusal to act, but resistance to abide. A person overcome by acedia may be quite busy—writing, serving, even ministering—but inwardly, there is no fire, no hunger, no movement toward God. The soul shrinks back from his presence, not in rebellion, but in fatigue. Not in outrage, but in indifference.

This is the temptation Screwtape so skillfully nurtures—not to shock the Christian into apostasy, but to lull him into spiritual inertia. If he can keep the soul distracted, passive, content with half-measures, dulled to beauty, and numbed to truth, he wins. The enemy's greatest victories are often not won in moments of dramatic failure, but in seasons of quiet drift.

---

4. See especially Evagrius Ponticus, *The Praktikos* (late 4th century), and John Cassian, *Institutes* (c. 426), for the early Christian diagnosis of *acedia* as a demonic temptation toward spiritual inertia and despair.

We know this experience. It doesn't arrive with fireworks. It slips in unnoticed. One day, prayer seems dry. Scripture feels distant. Worship becomes routine. Faith is no longer false, but it is no longer felt. We still confess, but the confession no longer stirs. We still believe, but belief no longer burns. We attend church but feel unmoved. We go through the motions while something vital dims inside.

Acedia is the soul's subtle surrender. It's not the loud betrayal of God's presence, but the quiet abandonment of his beauty. It doesn't argue with truth—it yawns at it. It doesn't hate holiness—it finds it exhausting. It doesn't resist the disciplines of grace—it avoids them, slowly, quietly, until they seem irrelevant. The heart begins to believe—without ever saying it out loud—that God is not worth the effort.

The danger of acedia is precisely this: it feels normal. It doesn't shock the conscience. It doesn't bring guilt. It hides under the disguise of tiredness or practicality. We tell ourselves we're just busy. That we need rest. That we'll get back to prayer tomorrow. But tomorrow becomes next week. And next week becomes never. And all the while, our spiritual senses dull. We become like a man who stops hearing the music playing in the background—not because it has stopped, but because his ears have grown used to the silence.

In the garden, the serpent's first words were not commands, but questions. "Did God really say?" The fall did not come by storm. It came by suggestion. Acedia is the same. It suggests that God is distant, his word is demanding, his presence is a weight. It tells us that a little distraction won't hurt, that prayer can wait, that intimacy with God is for another season of life. It gives us just enough religious habit to silence guilt, but not enough spiritual hunger to ignite joy.

This is lukewarmness. And our Lord speaks to it with holy severity. "Because you are lukewarm, and neither hot nor cold, I will spit you out of my mouth" (Rev 3:16). These are not the words of a harsh master but of a jealous lover. Christ desires our hearts, not our half-measures. Lukewarmness is not harmless—it is a refusal of love. It is a soul that once burned but now simmers, unwilling to

The Banality of Temptation

give itself fully, yet unwilling to walk away. It is a kind of spiritual coasting that is more dangerous than outright rebellion, because it deceives us into thinking we are fine.

But the truth is, we are not fine. Acedia is the quiet rot of the soul. It is not something we drift into harmlessly. It is the condition in which holy things lose their weight, and sacred things lose their wonder. And it can happen to any of us. It can happen to the preacher, the elder, the missionary, the mother, the student. It can happen when we're busy or when we're bored. It can happen even when everyone else thinks we're doing well. Because acedia does not first show itself in outward actions—it starts in the affections. It is a failure to desire. And the soul that no longer desires God is not neutral—it is dying.

Imagine a young father who once rose early to pray, Scripture open, heart expectant. In those early years of faith, he had tasted the joy of God's presence. Prayer was not a burden; it was breath. Scripture reading was not a duty; it was delight. But over time, the rhythm of daily life began to press in. Children needed tending. Work emails arrived earlier. Bills piled up. Church involvement increased, but not necessarily intimacy with Christ. Slowly, imperceptibly, his mornings of quiet devotion gave way to hurried glances at the clock. His Bible gathered dust while his calendar filled with meetings. He still believed, still confessed the creed, still attended church, and still taught his children to pray before meals. From the outside, nothing seemed wrong. But inside, something vital had dimmed.

He no longer expected to meet God—he simply managed life. The motions remained, but the fire faded. Worship became a ritual. Prayer became an afterthought. He told himself it was just a busy season, that he would return to God "when things settle down." But the drift had already begun—not into scandal or apostasy, but into the gray fog of acedia. Not into denial of the faith, but into a dull, passive, joyless endurance of it. He was no longer running the race but sleepwalking through it. And because everything looked fine externally, the danger went unnoticed. That is the quiet genius of acedia: it numbs without alarming, drains the soul without breaking the surface.

Screwtape's strategy is not always dramatic. Often, it is subtle: to lull a soul into contented distraction, to keep the affections cool and the will passive. And when that happens, the man who once burned with longing for God becomes a man who vaguely remembers what intimacy with God felt like—but no longer hungers for it. He has not renounced Christ, but neither does he seek him. He has not denied the truth, but he no longer trembles before it. He has become what the enemy most desires: a Christian in name, busy in service, outwardly stable, but inwardly asleep. This is not just the story of one man. It is the quiet crisis that threatens us all. And unless we are awakened by grace, we may never realize that we are drifting—not because we've stopped moving, but because we've stopped desiring.

What, then, is the way back?

The answer is not to do more, but to return. Not to perform, but to abide. Acedia cannot be overcome by frenzy or guilt. It must be healed by love. What the numb soul needs is not more obligation, but more of Christ. It is not a heavier burden, but a clearer vision of glory. The cure for sloth is not moral effort. It is the renewal of holy affection.

And that renewal begins in the ordinary. It begins with God's word opened when we don't feel like reading. It begins with the whispered prayer when our heart feels cold. It begins with showing up for worship when we'd rather stay home. It begins with asking God—not for better feelings, but for deeper hunger. This is how God works. He meets us not in our strength, but in our weakness.

There is no shortcut. No secret formula. Just the long road of grace. The daily turning of the heart. The quiet rhythms of obedience. The decision, again and again, to return to the one who alone gives life. The world tells us to follow our hearts. The gospel tells us to lead them—back to the cross, back to the empty tomb, back to the one who first loved us.

Acedia cannot stand in the presence of Christ crucified and risen. The love of Jesus cuts through the fog. The voice of Jesus calls the weary soul out of hiding. "Come to me," Jesus said, "all who labor and are heavy laden, and I will give you rest" (Matt 11:28). And the Spirit of Jesus breathes life where there was none. He does not wait for us to get it together. He meets us in the drift. He awakens what is dormant. He strengthens what is weak. He fans into flame what has gone cold.

And he does this again and again.

Because he is faithful.

Because he is gentle.

Because he knows that we are dust.

Discipleship, then, is not a heroic performance. It is a sustained surrender. It is not loud. It is not glamorous. It is daily. It is small. It is faith in the fog. It is love in the routine. It is the Spirit whispering in the silence: "You are mine." And the soul answering, even with trembling voice: "Yes, Lord. I'm still Yours." In other words, the battle against acedia is fought in the patterns of our lives—in the way we rise, in the way we pray, in the way we return to the Lord again and again. Because the grace of God is not only what saves us. It is what awakens us.

Chapter 4

Distraction as a Weapon

"You will find that anything or nothing is sufficient to attract his wandering attention. You no longer need a good book, which he really likes, to keep him from his prayers or his work or his sleep; a column of advertisements in yesterday's paper will do. You can make him waste his time not only in conversation he enjoys with people whom he likes, but in conversations with those he cares nothing about on subjects that bore him. You can make him do nothing at all for long periods." — *Screwtape*, Letter 13.

IF THE DEVIL CANNOT destroy your faith with doubt, he will drown it in noise. And distraction is one of the most powerful—and most underestimated—weapons in the enemy's arsenal. It is quiet. It is ordinary. It is everywhere. And that's precisely what makes it dangerous. Unlike temptation, which often appears as a moral crisis, distraction often presents itself as nothing at all. It has no shape, no urgency, no obvious threat. And yet, over time, it may do more to deform the Christian soul than open rebellion ever could.

For Screwtape, distraction is not simply a tactic—it's a lifestyle. The patient is gradually lured away from God not by wickedness, but by triviality. Screwtape doesn't demand that his subject fall into scandal. He just wants him to become spiritually forgetful. The genius of the demonic strategy, as Lewis presents it, is that the patient doesn't even realize it's happening. In Letter 13, Screwtape

DISTRACTION AS A WEAPON

laments the patient's temporary reawakening to grace, but he quickly pivots back to his strategy: keep him busy, unfocused, entertained. Let him skim headlines, scroll social media, stay up late doing nothing. Let him live distracted.

A SPIRITUAL THREAT HIDDEN IN PLAIN SIGHT

When we think about spiritual warfare, we tend to imagine something more dramatic: demon possession, moral collapse, or false teaching. But Lewis draws our attention to something far more ordinary and therefore more insidious: distraction. Distraction is spiritual warfare for the modern world. It doesn't shake your faith; it numbs it. It doesn't destroy belief; it dilutes it.

The devil's method, as Lewis reveals, is to turn every holy opportunity into a missed one—not through rage or blasphemy, but through what Screwtape calls "noise." In his universe, hell is "a kingdom of noise," and silence is a threat to be avoided at all costs. In Letter 4, Screwtape urges his nephew to prevent the patient from real prayer at all: "The best thing, where it is possible, is to keep the patient from the serious intention of praying altogether." The Christian who has "good intentions" to pray but never quite gets there, who opens the Bible app only to check email instead, who starts each day with vague spiritual thoughts but no focused communion with God—this is Screwtape's victory.

Distraction is not an interruption of the Christian life. It becomes the shape of it. Distraction, in its essence, is not just about attention. It's about formation. What we give our attention to, we give our hearts to. What we habitually focus on shapes what we love, what we value, and who we become. This is why distraction is never merely neutral. It is deeply formative.

The Scriptures have always warned of the danger of divided attention, not simply as a matter of mental focus but as a matter of spiritual allegiance. Attention is deeply formative—it shapes what we love, desire, and ultimately serve. This is why Paul exhorts the Colossians, "Set your minds on things that are above, not on things that are on earth" (Col 3:2). The implication is not that earthly responsibilities are unimportant, but that they must be ordered under the reign of Christ. A scattered mind, pulled in competing directions by worldly allurements, is easily drawn away from the single-hearted devotion that discipleship requires. Paul's call is to a disciplined reorientation of our inner life—what we look at, dwell on, and pursue.

In Romans 12:2, Paul returns to this theme with even greater force: "Do not be conformed to this world, but be transformed by the renewal of your mind." The contrast is sharp—either we are shaped by the world's patterns or transformed by God's truth. There is no neutral ground. The battleground of the mind is central to spiritual formation, because what we consistently attend to becomes what we believe and eventually what we obey. In this way, attention is not an afterthought in discipleship—it is the front line. In an age of distraction and digital overload, reclaiming our attention for God is not just wise; it is an act of spiritual resistance. To fix our eyes on Christ is to defy the gravitational pull of a world that would rather have us anxious, entertained, and ultimately disengaged from the things of God.

Yet we live in a world that competes for our attention at every moment. We check our phones before we check our hearts. We read notifications before Scripture. Our devices train us in constant novelty, and as a result, stillness becomes unbearable, and reflection feels unproductive. In such a context, prayer becomes labor, silence becomes threatening, and depth becomes rare. This is precisely what Screwtape wants. Not a rebellious sinner, but a distracted one. Not a bold denier of truth, but someone too busy to notice it.

FROM THE WIRELESS TO THE ALGORITHM: LEWIS'S PROPHETIC INSIGHT

When Lewis was writing in the early 1940s, the major sources of distraction included newspapers, radio broadcasts, war-time propaganda, and political anxieties. These were formidable enough.

But Lewis was already prophetically attuned to the coming temptation of an overstimulated mind.

In the twenty-first century, this danger has grown exponentially. Today's distractions are not random or circumstantial—they are manufactured and monetized. The smartphone is not merely a communication device; it is a personalized distraction engine. Notifications, social media feeds, algorithm-driven content—these are not just conveniences. They are spiritual competitors. As one author put it, we are now "amusing ourselves to death" through a thousand forms of digital indulgence.5 And all of it works in favor of Screwtape's goals. A soul perpetually distracted is a soul perpetually delayed in attending to God.

The modern Christian must recognize that the spiritual life now requires a kind of conscious rebellion against the ambient noise of culture. It is no longer possible to live a life of default discipleship. The flow of contemporary life will not carry the soul toward Christ. It will carry it toward fragmentation, shallowness, and forgetfulness of God. Distraction is the current, and we are called to swim against it.

THE INWARD TURN: HOW DISTRACTION DISGUISES ITSELF AS INTROSPECTION

One of Screwtape's most insightful strategies appears in Letter 4, where he recommends that the patient be encouraged to judge his prayers by their emotional impact. Rather than truly communing with God, the patient should be subtly taught to focus on whether he feels spiritual, or whether he can generate a mood of devotion. Screwtape writes, "Teach them to estimate the value of each prayer by their success in producing the desired feeling... Let them focus on themselves instead of on the Enemy [God]." This advice is chilling in its familiarity. How often do we equate spiritual success with emotional resonance? How often are we tempted to evaluate our

---

5. Neil Postman, *Amusing Ourselves to Death* (1986).

prayers based on how they made us feel, rather than whether we sought the face of God?

This is distraction in its most disguised form—disguised not as entertainment or urgency, but as sincerity. The soul is not turned away from God with a shout, but with a sigh, too preoccupied with its own internal state to look up and behold the beauty and glory of the Lord. We believe we are being reflective when in fact we are simply self-absorbed. Instead of lifting our hearts in worship or pouring them out in lament, we fall into an emotional loop, asking, "Am I really connecting with God?" without ever actually directing our minds and hearts to him. True prayer becomes impossible because God has been displaced from the center.

Screwtape's strategy here echoes the original temptation in Eden: to make man believe that he is the center of his own world, that spiritual reality is defined by how he feels rather than by the objective presence and promises of God. Eve is tempted not by open rebellion, but by a distorted desire—to become wise in her own eyes, to take her spiritual condition into her own hands. The turn inward, when untethered from trust in God, always leads to a collapse of perspective. Likewise, in the wilderness, when the Israelites faced hunger and fear, they didn't cry out to the God who had just delivered them from Egypt—they turned inward, grumbling, catastrophizing, and forgetting the mighty hand that had redeemed them (Exod 16:2–3). Distraction, in this sense, is often a failure of memory and trust.

The Psalms, by contrast, model a better path. When David feels overwhelmed or abandoned, he does not spiral into himself—he lifts his eyes: "Why are you cast down, O my soul, and why are you in turmoil within me? Hope in God; for I shall again praise him" (Ps 42:5). Even in the midst of deep introspection, the psalmist disciplines his attention. He questions his feelings, but he does not obey them. He remembers God's steadfast love, his past faithfulness, his covenant promises. This reorientation—away from the self and toward the Lord—is the lifeline for the distracted soul. It reminds us that the heart of the Christian life is not emotional clarity but covenantal communion.

DISTRACTION AS A WEAPON

In the New Testament, we see this inward preoccupation challenged by Jesus. In Luke 18, he tells the parable of the Pharisee and the tax collector. The Pharisee, though outwardly religious, is inwardly curved in on himself: "God, I thank you that I am not like other men..." (Luke 18:11). His prayer is less communion with God and more spiritual self-assessment. The tax collector, by contrast, simply pleads for mercy. He does not try to feel holy—he simply entrusts himself to the mercy of God. Jesus concludes that it is the tax collector who goes home justified. In this, we see the heart of spiritual warfare: not in the mastery of feelings, but in the surrender of the self. The inward turn must give way to the upward gaze. Only then can we resist the devil's whispered invitation to make ourselves the center of our own spiritual universe.

THE DEVASTATION OF THE PRESENT MOMENT

In Letter 15, Screwtape identifies a particularly dangerous concept: the present. In the present, the Christian is most able to encounter God, to receive grace, to hear the Spirit. "He would therefore have them continually concerned either with eternity (which means being concerned with Him) or with the Present," Screwtape writes, "because the Present is the point at which time touches eternity." This is the battleground. The devil's aim is to keep us anywhere but here. He pushes us toward nostalgia for the past or anxiety about the future—because either of those removes us from the only place God is truly found: the now.

Screwtape's tactic is not to steal faith but to postpone it. Not to banish prayer, but to delay it. Not to incite hatred of God, but to cultivate forgetfulness of him. The longer the soul remains distracted from the present moment, the further it drifts from the God who reveals himself in it. We have all experienced this—days that pass in a blur, with little thought of God; prayers offered without heart; conversations where we are physically present but spiritually absent. What Lewis reveals is that such states are not simply unfortunate—they are actively fostered by the forces of evil.

The war for our attention, then, is not a metaphor. It is real. It is theological. And it is raging.

Scripture is replete with the call to live attentively in the present, where God meets his people. When God reveals his name to Moses, he does not say, "I was" or "I will be"—He says, "I AM" (Exod 3:14). His presence is not a concept to be remembered or a promise to be anticipated alone—it is a reality to be encountered now. Jesus echoes this when he teaches his disciples to pray, "Give us this day our daily bread" (Matt 6:11), anchoring our dependence in the present tense. He also commands, "Do not be anxious about tomorrow, for tomorrow will be anxious for itself" (Matt 6:34). The kingdom of God is not some distant reality to be scheduled into our calendars; it is at hand (Mark 1:15). The enemy's goal is to obscure that truth by keeping us preoccupied with what cannot be controlled or changed.

Theologically, the present moment is not just an empty interval between past and future—it is a sacramental space, a window through which eternity breaks into time. Each moment carries the potential to become a means of grace: a word of encouragement, a whispered prayer, a small act of obedience, or even a breath of silent awe. This is why Paul commands believers to "make the best use of the time, because the days are evil" (Eph 5:16). Every moment surrendered to distraction is a moment surrendered to the enemy. But every moment reclaimed—by faith, gratitude, and attentiveness—is a small act of spiritual defiance. It is a declaration that Christ reigns not only over our theology, but over our time. The call, then, is clear: wake up, pay attention, and be present. For God is here.

ATTENTION AS A SPIRITUAL DISCIPLINE

What Screwtape fears most is not the intellectual Christian, the zealous activist, or the well-intentioned believer. What he fears is the attentive Christian—the one who lives in the present, who meets God in silence, who perseveres in unseen prayer, who is content to sit at Jesus' feet and listen (Luke 10:39). In an age of

Distraction as a Weapon

noise, hurry, and distraction, attention becomes a rare and radical act. It is a sign of resistance, a refusal to be conformed to the shallow rhythms of the world. The attentive Christian is not easily manipulated by emotional waves or cultural trends. Their eyes are fixed. Their heart is quiet. Their soul is watchful.

Such attention is not natural. It must be formed. It is, in the words of the ancient church, a spiritual discipline—a virtue cultivated by practice, by liturgy, by repentance, by returning again and again to the presence of God. The early Christians spoke often of *nepsis*, or watchfulness—being awake to the movements of the soul, alert to the voice of the Spirit, and guarded against the whispers of temptation.6 Attention, in this sense, is not passive but active. It is the patient training of the mind and heart to dwell where Christ is, to "set your minds on things that are above" (Col 3:2), and to abide in him moment by moment.

The attentive soul is a threat to hell. It cannot be manipulated by noise. It does not mistake emotion for truth. It sees through the fog of urgency and remembers what matters. It fixes its eyes not on what is seen, but on what is unseen, "for the things that are seen are transient, but the things that are unseen are eternal" (2 Cor 4:18). When attention is rightly ordered, it becomes clarity of vision, a lamp to the body (Matt 6:22). Such clarity allows the Christian to live with eternal purpose in a world obsessed with the immediate and superficial.

---

6. The concept of *nepsis*—spiritual watchfulness or sobriety—is deeply rooted in the patristic tradition. Evagrius Ponticus presents *nepsis*—watchfulness—as the essential discipline for guarding the heart from tempting thoughts, laying the foundation for Christian asceticism through careful attention to the inner life (*Praktikos* 6–14). John Cassian carries this tradition into the Latin West, urging vigilance over one's thoughts and desires as the path to purity of heart and unceasing prayer; he recounts the teaching of Abba Moses that "the soul cannot be cleansed unless it gives heed each day to its thoughts" (*Conferences* 1.20). Likewise, John Climacus emphasizes this same spiritual sobriety in *The Ladder of Divine Ascent*, describing watchfulness as "a continual fixing and halting of thought at the entrance to the heart" (*Ladder* 26.1). These early witnesses show that *nepsis* was not a marginal idea but a vital element of Christian discipleship from the earliest centuries.

Discipleship and Spiritual Warfare

Attention is the doorway to love. What we attend to, we learn to love. And what we love, we are shaped by. This is why Jesus calls his disciples to abide in him—not just once, but continuously (John 15:4–5). Abiding requires attention: to his word, his presence, his voice. It means staying close, remaining alert, and refusing to wander. The world will try to fragment our hearts, to scatter our desires, and to hijack our focus. But the path of discipleship calls us to gather ourselves in Christ, to behold him with unveiled face, and to be transformed from one degree of glory to another (2 Cor 3:18). In this way, the discipline of attention becomes the beginning of true formation. In attending to Christ, we become like him.

PASTORAL-THEOLOGICAL REFLECTION

Distraction is not a new danger, but it has taken on a terrifying clarity in our age. Screwtape understood its power. He boasted that he could keep his "patient" from prayer or sleep not by some grand temptation, but by a column of advertisements in yesterday's paper. How much more, then, in our present world? If a newspaper could derail the soul, what about a phone that pings every ten seconds, an endless scroll of curated images, and a culture designed to keep us addicted to novelty? The brilliance of Lewis's insight is that he saw distraction not merely as an inconvenience, but as a strategy of spiritual warfare.

The danger of distraction is not only that it consumes our time, but that it fragments our soul. It trains us to live on the surface of things. It makes attentiveness feel impossible. It weakens prayer, sabotages study, and erodes worship. It is not neutral. It is war. The scattered mind is not simply a psychological inconvenience—it is a spiritual vulnerability. Screwtape rejoices when we multitask our way through the holy. He does not care what we are looking at, as long as we are not looking at Christ.

In an age like ours, where the trivial masquerades as urgent and the urgent is drowned in noise, distraction becomes a weapon of mass spiritual dullness. It deadens wonder. It numbs the

Distraction as a Weapon

affections. It makes eternal things feel irrelevant and temporary things feel ultimate. It is not that we cease to believe in God, but that we forget why he matters. The mind is pulled in a thousand directions until the heart forgets its home.

This is why distraction is more than a modern inconvenience. It is a theological crisis. We are not simply overstimulated; we are disoriented. The very faculties we need to follow Christ—attention, imagination, memory, desire—are slowly being hijacked. In a world where nothing holds our gaze for long, how can we fix our eyes on Jesus? In a world of endless noise, how can we hear the still, small voice?

The call to discipleship is, at its core, a call to attention. "Let us fix our eyes on Jesus, the author and perfecter of our faith" (Heb 12:2). To attend to him is to live. To drift from him is to die. That is why the ancient practices of the Christian life are not optional. They are acts of war. Prayer is not merely a quiet moment; it is a resistance to the tyranny of the urgent. Scripture reading is not information-gathering; it is soul-shaping. The Christian sabbath is not a quaint tradition; it is a holy rebellion against the world's demands. Solitude is not emptiness; it is space for God to speak.

The enemy does not need to destroy our faith with arguments. He only needs to distract us long enough that we never truly gaze upon Christ. That is why the erosion is so effective. We do not fall by denying God outright, but by crowding him out. Slowly. Daily. Unthinkingly. We give our best attention to what is loudest, not what is truest. We drift not because we hate God, but because we forgot to remember him.

Consider a young woman who once treasured her morning time with God—a lit candle, a worn Bible, and the quiet hum of early light before the world intruded. But now, her alarm is the buzz of notifications. Before her feet touch the floor, her mind is already scrolling—emails, messages, headlines, weather, a dozen curated images. She tells herself she'll read Scripture after breakfast, then after she checks her calendar, then maybe during lunch. But the minutes slip away. She is not rebellious. She is simply overwhelmed. Not defiant, just distracted. Her soul is slowly being trained to crave interruption. To need the noise. And without realizing it, her inner life becomes as fragmented as her attention. She still believes. She still prays—briefly, distractedly. She still loves Jesus, but struggles to look at him for more than a moment. And when she finally sits down to pray, silence feels unbearable. Stillness feels foreign. Her thoughts dart. Her heart races. She reaches for her phone without meaning to. And the tragedy is not just that she has lost time, but that she is losing the capacity to attend to what is holy.

This is the crisis of distraction. It is not merely a technological or psychological problem—it is a theological one. Distraction is not just stealing our time; it is reshaping our souls. It forms us to live at the surface, to skim rather than dwell, to react rather than reflect. In doing so, it dulls our hunger for God and deadens our capacity for worship. We become spiritually malnourished not because we stopped believing, but because we stopped beholding. Screwtape does not need us to renounce Christ; he only needs to keep our eyes elsewhere. He rejoices when we multitask through prayer, skim Scripture, or hear sermons while checking sports scores. He knows that a scattered mind cannot dwell in the presence of God, and a distracted heart will never burn with love for Christ. Distraction, then, is not a passive condition—it is a spiritual battlefield. The call to fix our eyes on Jesus is not poetic advice; it is an act of war.

But the gospel breaks through even here. Christ does not leave us in our fragmentation. He calls us to himself. "Come to me... Learn from me..." (Matt 11:28–29). The invitation is not just to stop doing, but to start attending. To learn the way of rest. To recover the joy of presence. To center our attention not on what is flashy, but on what is eternal.

Therefore, to fight distraction is to remember who God is—holy, sovereign, gracious—and who we are as his image-bearers, redeemed by Christ and called to live in fellowship with him. It is to remember why we were made: to glorify God and enjoy him forever. In other words, to resist distraction is not merely a mental exercise, but a spiritual reorientation. It is to live *coram*

Distraction as a Weapon

Deo—a Latin phrase meaning "before the face of God." This ancient expression captures the essence of the Christian life: living every moment, in every place, with the awareness that we stand constantly in God's presence. To live *coram Deo* is to reject the divided life, where faith is kept separate from ordinary routines. Instead, it calls us to wholehearted, undivided devotion—whether in worship, work, rest, or relationships—knowing that all of life is sacred when lived before the one who sees and knows us fully. And in that posture, we begin to see again. We see that God is near. That our days are holy. That our work matters. That our worship shapes us. That our lives are not fragments, but a calling.

In a fragmented world, attention becomes an act of worship. And in that worship, we recover our humanity, our mission, and our joy. This is not a matter of personality or temperament. It is the necessary discipline of the disciple. Discipleship is attentiveness to Jesus. Anything that draws our eyes from him must be resisted. Not just because it is harmful—but because he is better.

The way forward is not in heroic effort but in holy habits. Not in digital detoxes alone, but in spiritual reorientation. The gospel does not offer a productivity system. It offers a Person. To look to him is to see everything else rightly. The cross brings clarity. The resurrection restores vision. The ascension anchors our attention where Christ is, seated at the right hand of God. We do not fight distraction alone. We follow the one who never lost sight of the Father.

So, fix your eyes. Look up. Pay attention. The world may buzz and blur, but Christ is steady. In him, the scattered soul finds center. The distracted heart finds peace. The disciple, once again, learns to listen. And to follow.

Chapter 5

Affections and Formation

"All mortals tend to turn into the thing they are pretending to be. This is elementary." — *Screwtape,* Letter 10.

AT THE HEART OF every act of obedience or sin, every moment of discipleship or drift, is love. Not just the romantic kind, not just the sentimental kind, but the deep, orienting force of the soul—the affections. What we love most, we move toward. What we desire most, we are shaped by. And that is precisely why the battle of spiritual warfare is, at its core, a battle for the heart.

In the *Screwtape Letters,* temptation is rarely reduced to bad behavior. It's about misdirected affections—subtle shifts in love, loyalty, and desire. Screwtape knows that if he can change what the patient loves, he can change who the patient becomes. This is one of the most profound spiritual truths: sin is not just about doing bad things; it's about loving good things wrongly. And discipleship, then, is not just about believing the right things—but loving the right things in the right order.

THE WAR FOR THE HEART

In Letter 10, Screwtape gleefully observes that the patient has made some new fashionable friends—worldly, self-satisfied people with clever opinions and light consciences. It is not that these friends are wicked, per se. It is that they are spiritually trivial. Screwtape's advice to Wormwood is simple: encourage the patient to keep up appearances. Let him say what's needed to fit in. Let him hide his faith in order to preserve social standing. "All mortals tend to turn into the thing they are pretending to be," Screwtape quips, "This is elementary."

The implication is chilling. We become what we imitate. The soul is malleable. It is shaped by what it admires and aligns with. Pretending leads to becoming—not just in the moral sense, but in the affective one. The more we attach our hearts to worldly approval, the more we become people for whom such approval is ultimate. Our affections solidify around our performances. We become the person we perform, because we learn to love what we think we need.

This is why Screwtape does not urge Wormwood to make the patient denounce Christianity. That's far too blunt. It might alert the patient to the stakes of the spiritual battle. Better to let him love something else a little more—his reputation, his wit, his clever new friends. Better to shift his affection slightly, imperceptibly, until the cross is no longer central but peripheral. Until Jesus is no longer beloved, but merely respected.

Lewis is drawing here from a long-standing Christian tradition, one that understands sin and sanctification not primarily in behavioral or intellectual terms, but in terms of disordered loves. As Augustine wrote, "living a just and holy life requires one to be capable of an objective and impartial evaluation of things: to love things, that is to say, in the right order, so that you do not love what is not to be loved, or fail to love what is to be loved, or have a greater love for what should be loved less, or an equal love for things that should be loved less or more, or a lesser or greater love for things that should be loved equally."[1] It is not wrong to love family, vocation, reputation, rest, or beauty. The problem is how we love them—when we love them more than the God who gives them.

---

1. Augustine, *On Christian Doctrine*, I.27-28

Discipleship, then, is not merely the acquisition of right doctrine or the performance of right duties—it is the reordering of the heart in the midst of a battle. It is spiritual warfare at the level of our affections, where we learn to love what is truly lovely and to desire what leads to eternal joy rather than the fleeting applause of the world. To follow Christ is to fight for a heart fully captivated by him.

THE AFFECTIONAL LANDSCAPE OF THE SOUL

Lewis returns again and again to the idea that humans are driven more by unconscious loves than by conscious thoughts. Screwtape is delighted when the patient's affections shift toward comfort, status, or self-pity—especially if he doesn't notice. "It's funny how mortals always picture us as putting things into their minds," he says in Letter 4. "In reality our best work is done by keeping things out." But what the demons keep out, in many cases, is love—love for God, for truth, for neighbor. And what they smuggle in are counterfeit loves—safety, pride, approval, indulgence. Screwtape does not need to supply heresy. He only needs to shift desire.

This becomes most obvious when Lewis explores romantic and sexual desire in the later letters. Screwtape loathes the idea of Christian love shaped by purity and permanence. In Letter 20, he advises Wormwood to distort the patient's longings by encouraging him to desire either the "alluring" or the "vapid"—women who will either excite lust or indulge vanity. The goal is to keep the patient's romantic ideals shallow, selfish, and ultimately destabilizing.

But Lewis is not denigrating human love. Quite the opposite. He is insisting that our loves must be shaped by something greater than impulse or instinct. They must be formed—intentionally, communally, liturgically—so that we learn to desire what is worthy of being desired.

In this, Lewis anticipates much of what modern theologians have argued in recent years. We are not merely "thinking things" or "believing brains." We are loving creatures. And our loves are

Affections and Formation

shaped more by the rhythms and rituals of daily life than by abstract ideas. What we love most often reveals what we worship.2

For Lewis, the spiritual life is a reformation of the affections. It is the process of becoming a person who wants God—not merely out of duty or fear, but from delight. And the great challenge is that the devil does not always oppose this process directly. He simply tries to replace it with other, lesser loves.

ENVIRONMENT, HABIT, AND THE SLOW DRIFT OF DESIRE

One of Lewis's sharpest insights is that the heart is more influenced by environment than by argument. If Screwtape can surround the patient with people who mock faith, normalize pride, reward superficiality, and flatter vanity, then the battle is already half-won. The heart does not change in a vacuum. It changes in context. And context is often invisible.

In Letter 10, Screwtape rejoices when the patient becomes embarrassed by his Christian identity in front of his worldly friends. This embarrassment does not arise from theology, but from social pressure. The patient has not adopted a new doctrine—he has caught a new mood. He begins to feel that Christianity is somehow "offensive," or "embarrassing," or "a little too much." And because his affections are no longer firmly rooted, he begins to care more about social belonging than spiritual fidelity.

Lewis understood that sin does not always arise from the will. It often flows from the affections. What we love shapes what we choose. What we admire forms what we become.

This is why Screwtape prefers an environment of vague spirituality to one of explicit sin. Better for the patient to be around "nice" unbelievers who value good manners and clever speech than around bold sinners who might remind him of what's really

---

2. For a helpful articulation of how human beings are shaped more by what they love than by what they think, see James Smith, *Desiring the Kingdom* (2009), and *You Are What You Love* (2016); and Tish Harrison Warren, *Liturgy of the Ordinary* (2016).

at stake. A tepid, respectable worldliness is far more effective than wild rebellion. The former reshapes the heart without alerting the conscience. In other words, the world gets in not by argument, but by affection. Lewis is suggesting here what the Christian tradition has long taught: we are formed over time by what we love, and by what we allow to love us back. And when we fail to examine our affections—when we let our hearts drift without direction—we soon find ourselves becoming someone we never intended to be.

WHAT SCREWTAPE FEARS

What then, according to Screwtape, is most dangerous to the devil's work? It is not a sudden burst of intellectual brilliance, nor even an emotional experience. It is a slow, deliberate reorientation of the heart's desire. It is when the patient begins to long for God—not for his gifts, but for his presence. When he begins to enjoy Scripture, not just as a duty, but as a delight. When he begins to choose the good, even when it costs him something. When love for Christ outweighs love for self. That is when Screwtape trembles.

Lewis is clear: the devil's strongest weapon is not rage—it is redirection. He doesn't need to destroy our faith. He only needs to steal our affection. Because once our hearts are captured by something else—comfort, control, image, ambition—then even orthodox theology becomes inert.

True Christian formation, then, is the formation of holy love. And such formation does not happen overnight. It happens through habits of worship, liturgies of grace, communities of truth. It happens as we behold the beauty of the Lord. We become what we love, and we love what we repeatedly give our attention to. Formation is not a flash of insight but a slow burning fire—fueled by prayer, Scripture, fellowship, repentance, and the sacraments.

This kind of formation requires patience, because God is not merely interested in changing our behavior—he is reshaping our hearts. He is weaning us from the world's shallow affections and retraining our desires to find their rest in him. The Spirit's work is not rushed. It often takes place in hidden, quiet places—in morning devotions, in the gathered worship of the church, in the ordinary choices of faithfulness. These small acts, repeated over time, become channels through which holy love is formed, deepened, and secured. This is the path of discipleship: not dramatic transformation in a moment, but daily surrender to the slow and sanctifying love of God.

PASTORAL-THEOLOGICAL REFLECTION

Screwtape is not afraid of doctrine. He is not concerned about church attendance, religious habits, or even theological conversation—so long as they remain disconnected from the heart. What he fears is not a well-informed Christian, but a well-formed one. He knows that human beings are not ultimately shaped by what they know, but by what they love. This is why he doesn't waste time trying to refute the truth; he seeks instead to reroute the affections. If he can seduce the soul to love reputation, comfort, or aesthetic experiences more than Christ, the battle is already won. This is not destruction by argument but deformation by delight.

The brilliance of Lewis's insight is that it cuts through both sentimentalism and intellectualism. It is not enough to feel something vaguely spiritual, nor is it enough to affirm the right theological categories. The real battleground is the heart—not the shallow place of fleeting emotion, but the deep center of our desires, inclinations, and loves. Scripture names this as the core of human identity: "Keep your heart with all vigilance, for from it flow the springs of life" (Prov 4:23). Jesus does not locate sin merely in behavior, but in affection: "From within, out of the heart of man, come evil thoughts" (Mark 7:21).

The enemy knows this. He knows that we become what we love. And he subtly trains us to love the wrong things in the wrong way. This is why the formation of desire is not a side project of the Christian life—it is the Christian life. Augustine said it long ago: "My love is my weight; wherever I go, my love is what moves

DISCIPLESHIP AND SPIRITUAL WARFARE

me."3 To be human is to be directed by desire. The question is not whether we will love, but what we will love—and how.

Imagine a seminary student who has mastered the theological categories. He can explain the *ordo salutis*4, debate the nuances of justification and sanctification, and quote several theologians with ease. He leads a Bible study, volunteers at church, and is known for his doctrinal precision. But if you were to observe his life closely, you might notice a subtle disconnection. His prayers are brief and mechanical. His worship is more concerned with musical excellence than the majesty of God. He is more grieved by theological imprecision than by his own impatience or pride. He talks about grace fluently, but rarely speaks of Jesus with affection. In truth, his loves have been quietly rerouted. He does not love falsehood—but neither does he burn with love for Christ. What motivates him is not communion with God, but admiration from others. He is doctrinally sound and spiritually stagnant. This is precisely what Screwtape desires: not a heretic, but a hollow Christian. A man who knows the truth but no longer trembles before it. A man who defends orthodoxy but has forgotten beauty. A man who has been deformed—not by false doctrine, but by disordered delight.

This is the battleground Lewis so brilliantly uncovers: not merely what we think, but what we love. The enemy is not afraid of bookshelves full of theology or churches filled with liturgy—as long as the heart remains untouched. He knows that real transformation happens not when minds are informed, but when hearts are re-ordered. And Screwtape's strategy is to subtly seduce us toward lesser loves—toward reputation, comfort, success, aesthetics—anything that can quietly replace Christ as our supreme

---

3. Augustine, *Confessions* 13.9.

4. *Ordo salutis* is a Latin phrase meaning "the order of salvation." It refers to the logical (not chronological) sequence of steps in which the Holy Spirit applies the benefits of Christ's redemptive work to the believer. Classic formulations in Reformed theology include elements such as election, effectual calling, regeneration, conversion (faith and repentance), justification, adoption, sanctification, and glorification. Though the exact order may vary among theological traditions, the *ordo salutis* helps clarify how different aspects of salvation relate to one another in the life of the believer.

AFFECTIONS AND FORMATION

treasure. The tragedy is that it often works, not because we stop confessing truth, but because we stop desiring the one who is true.

Theological formation that ignores the affections produces brittle disciples. But affectional formation rooted in truth produces saints.5 This is the aim of discipleship: not just to instruct, but to reorient. Not just to fill the mind, but to tune the heart. The gospel doesn't simply correct our ideas; it transforms our loves. And this transformation is not mechanical, but mystical. It is the work of the Spirit, who awakens in us a longing for Christ that no lesser thing can satisfy.

This is why the Christian life must be built around the means of grace. They are not merely tools of information, but instruments of spiritual formation. When God's word is preached, the heart is not merely taught—it is summoned. When the sacraments are received in faith, the soul is nourished with more than memory—it is nourished with grace. When the church worships, we are not engaging in religious performance—we are being re-formed in the presence of the living God.

The practices of the Christian life are not ways of earning grace, but ways of receiving it. They train our hearts to beat in rhythm with heaven. They reshape our desires over time, not in a moment of emotional intensity, but through faithful repetition. The Spirit uses these practices to lead us deeper into love, not just deeper into knowledge. Because the goal is not merely comprehension. The goal is communion.

And this communion changes us. We become what we behold. We are conformed to the image of what we adore. That is why the greatest threat to the Christian life is not failure or doubt,

---

5. For a theological account of the affections in Christian formation, see Jonathan Edwards, *Religious Affections* (1746), where Edwards argues that "true religion" consists primarily in "holy affections" stirred by the Spirit. Similarly, Augustine's *Confessions* presents the human heart as a restless organ, shaped and satisfied only by love for God: "You have made us for yourself, O Lord, and our heart is restless until it rests in you" (*Confessions* I.1). Together, these voices affirm that Christian formation must address the affections—those deep desires and loves that drive the will—not just the intellect, and that such transformation is the supernatural work of the Holy Spirit.

but misplaced affection. To love a good thing more than God is to distort both. And Screwtape knows it. His strategy is not to replace God with evil, but to replace him with almost anything else. Let the patient love music, or nature, or friendship, or romance, so long as these gifts are enjoyed apart from their giver. Let the heart be full of warmth, so long as it is not full of worship.

But God is not fooled. And his Spirit does not leave us to wander. He awakens our hearts again and again. He exposes the smallness of our loves and offers something better: himself. He teaches us not only what to reject, but what to adore. He forms in us holy affections—affections that are stable, true, and good.

This is why discipleship must be understood as the redirection of desire. It is not behavior modification. It is not cognitive mastery. It is the transformation of what we treasure. To love rightly is to live rightly. And this kind of love can only be formed in the presence of Christ, through the rhythms of grace, in the communion of saints.

The church, then, is not merely a classroom. It is a workshop of worship. A community where the heart is shaped and reshaped to delight in what is true, good, and beautiful. Where we learn, slowly and steadily, to love what God loves and to hate what he hates. Where doctrine and doxology meet. Where liturgy becomes life.

And this is the kind of life Screwtape cannot comprehend. A life shaped not by impulse, but by holy affection. A heart that beats for Christ. A soul formed by the gravity of grace. Because in the end, we become what we love. And if we love Christ, we become like him.

The enemy knows this. And he trembles.

Chapter 6

Prayer and Resistance

"The best thing, where it is possible, is to keep the patient from the serious intention of praying altogether." — *Screwtape*, Letter 4.

FEW SUBJECTS RECEIVE MORE strategic attention than prayer. From Screwtape's perspective, nothing is more dangerous than a believer who truly prays. Not because prayer is magical or manipulative, but because it draws the soul into communion with the living God. And in the fog of spiritual war, real communion is the one thing hell cannot counterfeit or conquer.

Screwtape's strategy is clear: if you can't stop the patient from praying, then distort his prayers. Distract him. Keep him focused on his own feelings or trapped in abstraction. Let him think prayer is about performance, posture, or pious vocabulary. Just don't let him encounter God. Because, as Screwtape says bluntly in Letter 4, "Whenever they are attending to the Enemy Himself [God], we are defeated."

Lewis, with pastoral wisdom, shows us that prayer is not just a spiritual exercise—it is spiritual warfare. To pray is to resist. To pray is to take up arms against the lies of the enemy. To pray is to declare, in the midst of confusion, "You are God and I am not. Come quickly to help me."

Discipleship and Spiritual Warfare

PRAYER AS WARFARE

The apostle Paul writes in Ephesians 6 that the Christian is to "put on the whole armor of God." After describing the belt of truth, the breastplate of righteousness, the shield of faith, and the sword of the Spirit, he adds this: "praying at all times in the Spirit, with all prayer and supplication" (Eph 6:18). In other words, prayer is not a passive add-on. It is a weapon. It is how we hold the line.

The battlefield of the Christian life is rarely clear. There are days when God feels absent, when temptation feels overwhelming, when prayer feels like shouting into the wind. These are the moments Screwtape relishes. But they are also the moments where prayer matters most.

In Letter 8, Screwtape bitterly confesses that their cause is "never more in danger than when a human, no longer desiring, but still intending to do our Enemy's will, looks round upon a universe from which every trace of Him seems to have vanished—and still obeys." That is prayer as resistance. Not emotionally satisfying, not immediately transformative—but defiant, faithful, real.

Prayer in spiritual warfare is not always victorious in tone. Sometimes it's trembling. Sometimes it's silence. But it is always a declaration of dependence. It is always a statement that the disciple is not self-sufficient.

THE DISRUPTION OF REAL PRAYER

Screwtape is remarkably perceptive in how he tries to disrupt prayer. He does not suggest that Wormwood convince the patient that God isn't real or that prayer is nonsense. That would be too risky. It might provoke a crisis that awakens faith. Better, Screwtape says, to let the patient continue to pray—but poorly. Let his prayers remain vague, insipid, abstract. Let him speak to "a composite object," some mental image or projection, rather than the living God.

In Letter 4, Screwtape writes: "If you examine the prayer of even the most devoted people, you will find that it appeals to what they think God is like, rather than to what he has revealed himself to be." This tactic is devastating. It lures the Christian into a kind of prayer that is not relational, but imaginary. The patient may be praying to "God," but it is a god of his own design—a safe, agreeable, sentimental deity. This, Lewis suggests, is no true prayer at all. It is spiritual ventriloquism.

Real prayer, by contrast, forces the soul out of fantasy and into reality. It exposes the heart. It confronts the sinner with holiness, the sufferer with compassion, the doubter with truth. Real prayer is not always eloquent. Often, it is raw. But it is always personal. It is directed toward the triune God who is not what we imagine, but what he has revealed. This is precisely what the enemy dreads.

FEELINGS AS FALSE GUIDES

One of Screwtape's favorite tools for undermining prayer is emotional manipulation. He encourages Wormwood to make the patient evaluate his prayers by how they feel. If he feels spiritual, then the prayer was "successful." If he feels dry or distracted, then it was a failure. In this way, Screwtape keeps the soul tethered to subjectivity rather than to faith. Screwtape writes: "Teach them to estimate the value of each prayer by their success in producing the desired feeling. Never let them suspect how much success or failure in prayer depends on whether they are well or ill, fresh or tired, at that moment" (Letter 4).

Lewis is unmasking one of the most pervasive lies in modern Christian life: that spiritual maturity is measured by emotional experience. In an age obsessed with authenticity and feelings, we have subtly come to believe that unless we feel close to God, we aren't close to him. If we don't feel inspired in worship, we think we're doing it wrong. If our prayers feel dry or lifeless, we suspect they are worthless. This mindset creates a fragile faith—one that depends more on mood than on truth. But Scripture consistently reveals that God is present not just in the fire or the whirlwind, but also in the still small voice (1 Kings 19:11–13). His nearness is not always felt, but it is always real.

This insight aligns with Lewis's broader vision of discipleship as steady, often unremarkable faithfulness. Screwtape writes that "the prayers offered in the state of dryness are those which please Him best" (Letter 8). Why? Because they are pure acts of faith, not driven by reward or emotion, but by trust. Spiritual maturity is not about chasing highs—it is about learning to remain. It is about obeying when God seems silent, loving when the heart feels dull, praying when words feel empty. This is the training ground of real faith: not the mountaintop, but the valley; not the light of midday, but the long obedience in the dark.

That is why the enemy fears the Christian who prays anyway—who returns day after day, wordlessly if necessary, trusting that God is still there. This kind of Christian cannot be manipulated by fluctuating feelings. They are rooted, anchored in the truth of God's character and promises rather than the weather of the soul. Their spiritual life is not performance but perseverance. And in the end, that is where lasting transformation happens—not in moments of emotional clarity, but in the quiet decision to believe and obey when everything in us wants to give up. This is the heart of discipleship.

THE POSTURE OF THE BODY AND THE FOCUS OF THE MIND

One of the more surprising insights is Screwtape's disdain for physical posture in prayer. He warns Wormwood not to let the patient kneel or adopt any bodily position that reflects submission. "At the very least," Screwtape complains, "they can be persuaded that the bodily position makes no difference to their prayers; for they constantly forget, what you must always remember, that they are animals and that whatever their bodies do affects their souls" (Letter 4). What Lewis exposes here is profoundly theological: humans are not spirits trapped in bodies—we are embodied souls, integrated wholes. What we do with our bodies not only expresses but shapes what we believe and how we worship.

Prayer and Resistance

This may seem minor to modern ears—especially in a digital age where worship often occurs seated, distracted, or mediated through screens—but Lewis's point is an ancient one. Scripture never separates body from soul in the way post-Enlightenment culture tends to. In the Old Testament, posture matters. Abraham falls facedown when God speaks (Gen 17:3). Moses takes off his sandals before the burning bush (Exod 3:5). The psalmists speak of kneeling, lifting hands, clapping, dancing, even lying prostrate in awe (Ps 95:6; 63:4; 149:3). These gestures are not empty rituals—they are bodily responses to divine presence. They train the soul in reverence, dependence, and joy.

In the New Testament, we see the same physical attentiveness. Jesus himself falls on his face in Gethsemane (Matt 26:39). Paul exhorts believers to "present your bodies as a living sacrifice, holy and acceptable to God, which is your spiritual worship" (Rom 12:1). Worship is not merely an inward or intellectual act—it involves the whole self. To kneel in prayer, to bow the head, to raise one's hands—these are not theatrics but formative acts. They teach humility, gratitude, surrender. The body, far from being irrelevant to spirituality, is one of the primary instruments through which we express love and reverence to God.

This is precisely why Screwtape hates it. He prefers prayer to be vague, disembodied, sentimental, and passive. He delights when Christians pray without attention, worship without posture, or reduce faith to a mental checklist. But God calls us to holistic worship. He desires not just thoughts or feelings, but hearts and minds and bodies. In Mark 12:30, Jesus affirms the greatest commandment: "You shall love the Lord your God with all your heart and with all your soul and with all your mind and with all your strength." Strength is not metaphorical—it includes the physical self. To love God bodily is to offer him every part of our being in reverence and delight.

The modern Christian often neglects this truth. In an era of digital spirituality, where church is streamed and prayer is often internalized or privatized, we are tempted to think of our bodies as irrelevant or even distracting to spiritual life. But Scripture and tradition insist otherwise. The body is not a hindrance to prayer—it is a vessel for it. Worship is enacted. Prayer is embodied. Our physical posture can cultivate spiritual posture. Just as kneeling helps humble the heart, standing in praise lifts the spirit. As Lewis reminds us through Screwtape's irritation, what we do with our bodies in prayer matters.

PRAYING IN THE FOG

The metaphor that best captures Lewis's vision of prayer is that of fog. The Christian life is often lived in murky terrain, where spiritual clarity is rare and temptation is near. As Paul writes, we are "seeing through a glass darkly" (1 Cor 13:12). In that fog, we cannot rely on sight. Feelings fluctuate, certainty fades, the world grows loud, and in such moments, prayer is not simply a spiritual discipline—it is a lifeline. It becomes not only a line of communication but a compass. It orients the soul toward God when all other bearings are lost. Prayer is the act of remembering where home is, even when the road disappears beneath our feet.

Screwtape wants the patient to forget this. He wants him to assume that prayer is for the clear days, the high moments—when the music swells, the sun is shining, and God feels near. He wants the Christian to believe that unless prayer feels good, it isn't real. He wants him to associate prayer with ease and abandon it when it becomes labor. But what he fears—what he dreads—is the Christian who learns to pray in the dark. The one who prays with dry lips and a weary mind, not because of emotional reward, but because they know the heavenly Father is listening. That kind of prayer—quiet, determined, even faltering—is a declaration of allegiance. It is love unmoored from feeling but rooted in faith.

When the patient continues to pray despite confusion or silence, Screwtape panics. Why? Because such prayer proves the presence of real faith—a faith not based on what is seen or felt, but on the character of God. Prayer in the fog is faith in action. It is not triumphant or eloquent, but it is immovable. It does not demand answers but chooses to remain. In that sense, real prayer

Prayer and Resistance

is not always articulate—it is often groaning, as Paul says, "with groanings too deep for words" (Rom 8:26). And the Spirit meets us there, praying for us, carrying our fragile faith into the throne room of grace. That kind of prayer, offered in darkness, is more powerful than a thousand words spoken in clarity.

This reminds me of what Bonhoeffer called "the cost of discipleship." It is easy to sing when the sun is shining. It is hard to pray in the valley of the shadow. But it is there—precisely there—that prayer becomes a shield. It is there that resistance becomes real. In the fog, Satan whispers, "God has abandoned you," and still the believer lifts a trembling voice heavenward. In that moment, heaven hears what hell dreads: not the strength of the prayer, but the resolve of the soul to pray at all. This is not the spirituality of spectacle or ease—it is the slow, silent courage of the saints.

Jesus models this perfectly. In Gethsemane, he prayed in agony, sweat mingling with blood, wrestling not only with death but with abandonment (Luke 22:44). And yet he prayed, "Not my will, but yours, be done." On the cross, his voice rang out in despair: "My God, my God, why have you forsaken me?" (Matt 27:46). But even then, he spoke to the Father. Even then, he clung to the bond of communion. Christ's prayers in the fog are not only our example—they are our hope. Because he prayed in darkness and prevailed, we too can pray in our own.

This is the invitation of prayer: not to have the right words, but to keep speaking to the right person. Not to have all the answers, but to refuse to walk alone. The goal of prayer is not emotional resolution but relational fidelity. God is not grading our eloquence—he delights in our persistence. Prayer is not a performance but an embrace, even when the arms tremble.

This is the essence of resistance. In a world that constantly pulls the soul away from God, prayer is how we hold the line. It is not always triumphant. Often, it is fragile. But even a fragile prayer, sincerely offered, is an act of spiritual defiance. It is a small rebellion against despair, a quiet declaration that God is still God—even when we can barely say so aloud. That kind of prayer, however weak it feels, is a thunderclap in the halls of hell. When we pray in the fog, we proclaim the most powerful truth of all: that God is worthy of trust even when the path is hidden, the heart is heavy, and the heavens seem silent.

THE CHURCH AS A SCHOOL OF PRAYER

If prayer is warfare, then the church must be a training ground. We are not meant to learn to pray in isolation, as though prayer were a private hobby. We are meant to learn within the life of the church, among fellow soldiers of Christ who can help bear our burdens, lift our arms when we are weary, and teach us how to plead with God. In too many congregations today, prayer is peripheral. It is often brief, routine, impersonal—tacked on between announcements and the sermon, or rushed through as a transition. But this is a far cry from the pattern of the early church, which "devoted themselves to the prayers" (Acts 2:42). Corporate prayer was not merely ceremonial—it was formational. It was how the people of God stayed awake in the fight.

Prayer, in the early church, was not for the spiritually elite—it was the air everyone breathed. It taught them to rely not on their own strength but on the Spirit's power. In gathered prayer, hearts were united, burdens were shared, and spiritual boldness was renewed (Acts 4:31). Prayer reminded them that they belonged to God and not to Caesar. It tuned their hearts to the frequency of heaven. It gave voice to their longing for Christ's return and strength for their witness in the meantime. In other words, prayer was the furnace where Christian affections were forged and the battlefield where they learned to endure.

We need to recover this today. The church is not a club of the competent—it is a community of the needy. We do not gather because we have it all together but because we are constantly tempted, distracted, and weak. And prayer is how we confess that need—not just individually, but together. When we pray with and for one another, we are practicing mutual resistance. We are bearing one another's spiritual burdens and reinforcing each other's faith. One person's cry can lift the weary. Another's thanksgiving can revive the discouraged. In prayer, the body ministers to itself, and the Spirit ministers to all.

Prayer meetings are not the "optional extras" of church life—they are the war rooms. They are the places where disciples learn to speak truth back to the lies of hell, where doubt is named and confronted, and where hope is rekindled. In the age of distraction and despair, corporate prayer is an act of defiance. It trains us to listen for God's voice above the noise of the world. It prepares us to pray in the fog, to endure in the night, and to rejoice in the dawn. A praying church is a resilient church, a dangerous church. And it is in that kind of church that spiritual warriors are formed.

PASTORAL-THEOLOGICAL REFLECTION

Screwtape does not fear words. He fears prayer. He does not fear a Christian talking about God or even studying doctrine. What he fears is the soul that bends low before the living God, not in performance, but in dependence. Prayer, in Screwtape's hellish estimation, is dangerous. It cannot be easily controlled. It defies distraction. It reorients the soul. And above all, it invites God in. For this reason, Screwtape's advice to keep the patient from prayer is not merely tactical—it is theological. He knows that real prayer is not wishful thinking. It is not a mystical technique. It is a spiritual battle. When a Christian prays with intention, something eternal is at work. Heaven listens. Hell trembles.

Prayer, then, is not peripheral to the Christian life. It is the core of resistance. To pray is to declare that we are not sufficient unto ourselves. It is to break the spell of autonomy. It is to speak directly to the one who rules heaven and earth. In this sense, prayer is defiance. It resists the illusion that the visible world is all there is. It confesses, in a world obsessed with immediacy, that we believe in a God who hears, even when he is silent.

This is why prayer is difficult. Not because God is far, but because our hearts are often scattered. We approach God with flickering thoughts, distracted minds, and inconsistent desires. And yet—we are heard. Not because we pray well, but because God is good. Not because our words are eloquent, but because Christ is our intercessor.

This is the great threat to the kingdom of darkness: not polished prayers, but honest ones. Not rehearsed spirituality, but real dependence. This is the kind of prayer the devil dreads. Because this kind of prayer changes people. It humbles the proud. It strengthens the weak. It draws the heart away from empty things and toward the living God.

Picture a woman sitting alone in her car, weary from a long day—work deadlines, family tensions, and the low-grade anxiety that hums beneath the surface of modern life. She scrolls her phone instinctively, looking for a momentary distraction. But something unsettles her. She puts the phone down. She exhales. And then, without fanfare or eloquence, she whispers, "Lord, I can't do this without you." That quiet, honest cry—unfiltered and unpolished—is an act of profound defiance. In that moment, she has done something Screwtape fears more than anything. She has broken the illusion of self-sufficiency. She has turned her gaze from the flickering shadows of this world to the throne of grace. It wasn't a long prayer. It wasn't theologically complex. But it was real. And real prayer, even in fragments, shakes the foundations of hell.

This is why prayer is not merely a spiritual practice—it is a declaration of war. It is not a retreat into private spirituality, but an advance into the presence of God. Screwtape does not fear when we talk about prayer; he fears when we actually pray. He does not fear pious language; he fears dependence. Because real prayer reorients the soul. It recenters our desires. It breaks the spell of autonomy and reawakens the truth that we are creatures—needy, limited, desperate for grace. In a world that worships strength, prayer is weakness willingly confessed. In a world that demands performance, prayer is surrender. And in a world that prizes immediacy, prayer is patience. It says, even when heaven feels silent, "I still believe. I still trust. I still wait." This is why prayer is not optional. It is not a supplement to the Christian life. It is the lifeline. It is how we resist the devil. It is how we return to the Father. It is how we keep our hearts alive in a world designed to deaden them.

Prayer and Resistance

Throughout Scripture, the people of God are formed by prayer. Abraham intercedes. Moses pleads. Hannah weeps. David sings. Jesus withdraws. The early church gathers to pray. Paul urges believers to pray without ceasing, not because it is convenient, but because it is necessary. Prayer is the posture of the pilgrim. It is the lifeline of the disciple. It is not a mystical escape but a form of warfare. And the enemy will do anything to keep us from it.

That is why Screwtape encourages vague spirituality. He does not mind if the patient dabbles in inspiration, so long as he avoids the real presence of God. He does not mind if the Christian reads about prayer, thinks about prayer, talks about prayer—so long as he does not actually pray. But when a Christian does pray, even haltingly, something changes. The soul is drawn out of the fog. The self is de-centered and God becomes near. This is not because prayer manipulates divine action, but because it aligns human desire with divine reality. Prayer is not control. It is communion. And communion is always transformative.

The Reformation saw this clearly. Martin Luther called prayer "the most necessary work of the Christian," and John Calvin, "the chief exercise of faith." Calvin compares prayer to digging for a treasure. He says that we "dig up by prayer the treasures that were pointed out by the Lord's gospel, and which our faith has gazed upon."1 The Reformers didn't see prayer as optional. Both Luther and Calvin saw it as essential to the life of grace. Because prayer is not about informing God. It is about being formed by Him. It is where our desires are sifted, our pride is softened, and our trust is strengthened. Luther, in his *Large Catechism*, spoke of prayer as "the most necessary work of the Christian," insisting that "we should not in any way despise our prayer."2 Luther viewed prayer not as a meritorious work but as an act of childlike dependence on the Father. He affirms,

> Christians must be armed in order to stand against the devil. For what do you think has hitherto accomplished such great things, has checked or quelled the counsels,

---

1. Calvin, *Institutes*, 3.20.2
2. Luther, *Large Catechism*, III.124.

purposes, murder, and riot of our enemies, whereby the devil thought to crush us, together with the Gospel, except that the prayer of a few godly men intervened like a wall of iron on our side? They should else have witnessed a far different tragedy, namely, how the devil would have destroyed all Germany in its own blood. But now they may confidently deride it and make a mock of it; however, we shall nevertheless be a match both for themselves and the devil by prayer alone, if we only persevere diligently and not become slack.3

The truth is that prayer rarely feels triumphant. More often, it feels weak, mundane, interrupted. And that is precisely why it matters. It is not a performance. It is participation in the life of God. In a world where value is measured by results, prayer is an act of holy resistance. It trusts not in what is seen, but in the unseen hand of a faithful God.

So, we must learn to pray not because we are good at it, but because we are not. We pray not because it is efficient, but because it is essential. Prayer is the place where we stop pretending and start depending. It is not impressive. It is intimate. It is not glamorous. It is grounded. And that, more than anything, is what the enemy hates. Because when we pray, we remember. We remember who we are and who God is. We remember the promises. We remember the cross. We remember that we are not alone. And in that remembering, we are re-formed. Prayer pushes back the lies. It recenters our affections. It revives our weary hearts.

In a distracted world, to pray is to fix our attention. In a cynical world, to pray is to believe. In a hurried world, to pray is to wait. In a broken world, to pray is to hope. And in all of this, prayer becomes the very resistance Screwtape fears. Not because we are strong, but because God is. Prayer, therefore, does not make us invincible. It makes us faithful. It does not remove suffering. It brings us into the presence of the one who redeems it. And that presence is our strength. That presence is our peace.

No wonder Screwtape trembles.

---

3. Luther, *Large Catechism*, III.31.

Prayer and Resistance

Because a Christian on his knees is never weak.
He is armored.
He is seen.
He is heard.

Chapter 7

The Church as a Battleground

"One of our great allies at present is the Church itself."
— *Screwtape*, Letter 2.

IT MAY SEEM COUNTERINTUITIVE that Screwtape would call the church one of his "great allies." But that is precisely what makes the second letter so striking—and so revealing. The enemy, it turns out, does not need to keep the Christian out of church. He simply needs to distort what the Christian sees and experiences within it.

The church, as Lewis portrays it, is a battleground. Not because it is failing, but because it is essential. Not because it is corrupt, but because it is Christ's body. The church is the visible sign of God's redemptive work in the world, and therefore, it is a prime target of demonic sabotage.

Screwtape urges Wormwood not to prevent the patient from going to church but to make sure he focuses on the outward appearance of things: the squeaky voice of the person next to him, the eccentric clothing of the pastor, the awkwardness of the liturgy. Let the patient judge the church by the visible and forget the invisible. Let him think of the church as a human institution, not as a spiritual mystery. Let him see hypocrisy, not holiness. Division, not grace. Criticism, not communion.

This is the devil's tactic: to sow distrust, comparison, and cynicism in the very place God intends for sanctification, healing, and unity. If discipleship is the lifelong journey of being formed in Christ, then the church is the primary context where that journey unfolds. Which is why it becomes a primary site of spiritual warfare.

CHURCHGOING AS A TEMPTATION?

In one of the most striking reversals, Screwtape admits that a man going to church can be dangerous—for hell. If the patient insists on attending, then the enemy must shift tactics. Direct opposition may only strengthen his resolve, so the strategy becomes more subtle: distort the way he sees the church. Screwtape writes in Letter 2: "Provided that any of those neighbors sing out of tune, or have boots that squeak, or double chins, or odd clothes, the patient will quite easily believe that their religion must therefore be somehow ridiculous." This strategy is not to keep the patient from church but to keep him from worship. The man may be physically present but spiritually disengaged—attending with a critical heart, observing the faults of others, and missing the presence of God altogether.

This tactic is devastating precisely because it feels so harmless. Rather than confronting the patient with doctrinal objections or philosophical doubts, Screwtape simply points his attention to the people around him. Their singing, their posture, their awkwardness. And slowly, the man stops seeing the church as a gathering of God's redeemed and starts seeing it as a group of unimpressive, often irritating individuals. The tragedy is that the diagnosis isn't wrong—churches are full of broken, awkward, and inconsistent people. But what Screwtape wants is for the patient to stop seeing them as fellow sinners saved by grace and to see them instead as obstacles to his own spiritual progress. In doing so, pride is nurtured, humility is extinguished, and the communal nature of the Christian life is subtly severed.

Lewis exposes a basic but uncomfortable truth here: our expectations of the church are often too idealistic. We expect saints and find sinners. We long for the heavenly Jerusalem and find ourselves sitting beside people with bad breath and poor taste in hymns. The gap between our ideal of church and the reality of church becomes fertile soil for temptation. Disillusionment quietly turns to resentment, and resentment to detachment. The enemy doesn't need us to hate the church. He only needs us to view it with cold indifference—to remain in it physically while withdrawing emotionally and spiritually. This is how the heart begins to harden—not through scandal, but through slow, subtle critique.

Screwtape's genius lies in preventing the patient from seeing himself as one of those flawed people. Let him judge others harshly but excuse his own sins as quirks. Let him demand grace for himself while refusing to extend it to his neighbor. Let him hop from one church to another, always looking for the perfect expression of worship or community, but never staying long enough to be known, corrected, or changed. Lewis describes this as becoming a "taster" of churches—one who samples but never commits, who evaluates but never belongs. And in this way, Screwtape ensures that the man will avoid the very discomforts that lead to sanctification: confession, accountability, and faithful perseverance with other sinners.

THE MYTH OF THE "IDEAL" CHURCH

Screwtape's strategy of turning churchgoers into critics reflects Lewis's deep understanding of the modern pursuit of the "ideal" church—a pursuit that, far from being noble, is often spiritually corrosive. Screwtape approves of Christians who become ecclesial consumers, always searching for a church that "suits" them. He writes: "Provided that opinions are not acted on, or do not seriously affect practice, let the patient adopt any opinions whatever. The more 'spiritual' they are, the better… But the search for a suitable church makes the man a critic where the Enemy wants him to be a pupil" (Letter 16). This seemingly harmless quest becomes, in Screwtape's hands, a method of spiritual paralysis. Instead of growing through commitment, the patient is trapped in endless evaluation—always critiquing, never submitting; always visiting, never belonging.

Screwtape says, "Surely you know that if a man can't be cured of churchgoing, the next best thing is to send him all over the neighborhood looking for the church that 'suits' him until he becomes a taster or connoisseur of churches... The search for a 'suitable' church makes the man a critic where the Enemy wants him to be a pupil" (Letter 16).

Lewis is warning against the consumer mentality that evaluates churches the way one might evaluate restaurants or music playlists. "I like the preaching, but the worship is too emotional." "The theology is solid, but the coffee is bad." "The small groups are helpful, but the kids' ministry isn't what I hoped." When the church becomes a matter of personal taste, the focus shifts from God to self. Our criteria become individualistic and transactional. We cease to ask whether the church is faithful—faithful to the gospel, to the Scriptures, to the sacraments, to Christ—and instead ask whether it is comfortable, convenient, or entertaining. The danger is not that the church fails to meet our expectations, but that we start to believe our preferences should be central in the first place.

But the church, properly understood, is not a spiritual boutique. It is not a custom-tailored community built to fit our personalities or cultural sensibilities. It is the covenant people of God—called into being by the Father's election, centered on the Son's redeeming work, and sustained by the Spirit's presence. It is Christ's bride, not our personal brand. The church exists not to affirm our preferences but to shape our souls. And soul-shaping rarely happens through ease or aesthetic harmony. It happens through commitment, repentance, sacrifice, and perseverance. The Spirit often uses disappointment, friction, and even boredom to chisel away our pride and conform us to Christ. Church is not about finding the perfect fit—it's about being fitted to Christ through a community of imperfect saints.

The irony, as Screwtape knows all too well, is that the imperfect church is precisely the place where God's grace is most visibly and powerfully at work. The very things that make the church difficult—diverse personalities, broken relationships, clumsy leadership, unpolished worship—are the things that force us to grow in grace. They are not obstacles to spiritual formation; they are the crucible in which it happens. The church is where sinners are gathered, where wounds are exposed, where forgiveness is practiced, and where love must be exercised in real-life conditions—not imagined or idealized ones. This is the soil in which humility grows. This is where the Spirit forms people who look like Jesus. And this is why the devils hate it. Because a believer who stays, who commits, who endures—even when it's hard—is a believer being sanctified. And sanctification, slowly and surely, crushes the gates of hell.

HYPOCRISY AND THE SLOW WORK OF GRACE

Another favorite weapon in Screwtape's arsenal is the charge of hypocrisy. In Letter 2, he relishes the moment the patient finally joins a local church, only to be met by a congregation that fails to impress. Screwtape writes: "When he gets to his pew and looks round him he sees just that selection of his neighbors whom he has hitherto avoided." The devil's strategy is simple: cause the patient to mistake imperfection for inauthenticity. If the church is full of flawed people, then surely the faith they profess must be flawed as well.

This logic is devastating in its simplicity—and it has been repeated endlessly in modern culture. "I like Jesus, but not the church." "Christians are just hypocrites." "Why would I listen to people who don't practice what they preach?" These objections are often voiced with the sting of real hurt. Many who walk away from the church do so not out of intellectual doubt, but emotional disillusionment. And yet, beneath the pain often lies a dangerous misconception: the belief that the presence of sin in the church nullifies the truth of the gospel. But this misunderstands what the church is and how grace works. The gospel never claimed that Christians are flawless. It claims that we are forgiven—and being slowly, painfully, transformed.

The Church as a Battleground

The church is not a museum of virtue but a hospital for sinners. It is not made up of spiritual elites who have arrived, but of weary pilgrims still on the journey. The mark of a true Christian is not sinlessness, but repentance. Hypocrisy, in the biblical sense, is not the presence of sin, but the denial of it. Jesus reserved his harshest words for the Pharisees—not because they sinned, but because they pretended they didn't. There is a vast difference between a believer who struggles against sin and one who performs righteousness to maintain appearances. Most faithful Christians are not hypocrites; they are painfully aware of their failings and desperately clinging to the grace of Christ. They do not excuse their sin—they mourn it. They do not flaunt their holiness—they hunger and thirst for righteousness.

Screwtape's brilliance lies in making the patient expect sainthood from everyone else while excusing mediocrity in himself. Let him notice every flaw in others—their tone, their posture, their petty habits—but remain blind to his own pride, apathy, or self-righteousness. Let him forget that he, too, is a work in progress. Let him become a connoisseur of other people's sins, rather than a disciple growing in humility. And all the while, the enemy of his soul keeps him from entering into the very means of grace that would transform him. In doing so, the devil keeps the patient isolated from the refining furnace of real community—where sin is not ignored, but brought to light; where grace is not abstract, but embodied in confession, forgiveness, and love.

God's grace rarely works according to our timetable. It moves slowly, quietly, persistently—often beneath the surface. Sanctification is not a lightning bolt; it is a long obedience in the same direction. The New Testament uses earthy metaphors to describe it: growing like a tree (Ps 1), being refined like gold (1 Pet 1:7), being built like a house (Eph 2:19–22). These are not instantaneous processes. They are slow, sometimes painful, always patient. The church is not the showroom of finished saints—it is the construction site of new creation. Sunday after Sunday, through the ordinary means of grace—preaching, sacraments, singing, praying, confessing—God is shaping a people. Not into perfection all at once, but into holiness, bit by bit. Screwtape hates this, because he knows the truth: even a flawed church, filled with sinners clinging to Christ, is a greater threat to hell than a thousand isolated "spiritual" individuals who refuse to belong.

THE CHURCH AS THE PLACE OF REAL FORMATION

In one of the most insightful moments, Screwtape laments that if the patient insists on continuing to go to church, he should at least be encouraged to go disengaged. Let him show up, but stay closed off. Let him be passive—an observer rather than a participant. Let him consume the service like a critic at a theater, analyze the sermon for style instead of substance, judge the music by personal taste, and treat the prayers and sacraments as quaint traditions. Above all, let him avoid the dangerous possibilities of repentance, self-examination, or honest worship. Let him sit through the entire liturgy while thinking about how the sermon applies to his neighbor. This, Screwtape knows, is how the soul remains unchanged, even within the very means that God has appointed for transformation.

Here Lewis's ecclesiology comes into sharp focus. He does not idealize the church or pretend it is above reproach. He is fully aware of its flaws—its hypocrisy, its dullness, its personalities, its politics. But what makes the church holy is not the perfection of its people but the presence of its God. For Lewis, the church is not simply a spiritual institution; it is a sacramental reality—a place where heaven touches earth, not because of human excellence but because of divine promise. It is through the ordinary rhythms of gathered worship—the word preached and heard, the sacraments received in faith, the prayers of the saints, the singing of psalms and hymns, and the fellowship of believers—that God works to shape the soul. The church is the workshop of grace, the crucible of character, and the school of love.

Screwtape's goal, therefore, is to turn the church into something safe. Aesthetic. Familiar. Toothless. He would love nothing more than for the Christian to attend church every week and remain spiritually untouched—entertained but unmoved, informed but unrepentant. In this way, even the act of churchgoing can be weaponized against the believer. The tragedy is not the absence of church attendance but the absence of transformation within it. If church becomes a performance to watch, a community to network, or a tradition to maintain, then its power is blunted. But if the church is engaged rightly—even when it is unimpressive, even when the sermon is average and the music is off-key—it becomes holy ground. Because worship is not about emotional stimulation or intellectual curiosity. It is about encounter with the living God.

The real scandal of the church is not its sinfulness—we already expect that. The true scandal is that God, in his mercy, has chosen to dwell among sinners. He inhabits the praises of his people (Ps 22:3). He walks among the lampstands (Rev 2:1). He communes with his people through means that appear weak and foolish to the world: bread and wine, water and word, song and silence. And through these simple, sacred things, he conforms us to the image of his son. That is why the church matters. That is why it is worth showing up, even when we don't feel like it. Because every Sunday, through the ordinary and unimpressive, the Spirit is chiseling us—sometimes imperceptibly, sometimes painfully—into something eternal. And the enemy knows it.

PASTORAL-THEOLOGICAL REFLECTION

Screwtape counts the church among his "great allies." He delights when Christians attend worship while withholding their hearts, when they focus on quirks rather than grace, and when they expect the church to serve them rather than form them. His strategy is brilliant: exploit disappointment, stir up disillusionment, and turn the Christian from a worshiper into a critic. In so doing, Screwtape mocks the visible weaknesses of the church while obscuring its invisible glory. But Lewis, through his satire, invites us to see deeper. Beneath the flawed surface, the church is not just another institution. It is the battleground of spiritual formation and the object of divine affection.

The New Testament gives us no illusions. The church is a messy place. Paul writes to communities riddled with sin and dysfunction, and yet calls them saints. The believers in Corinth are divided, immature, and morally compromised—but Paul still greets them as "the church of God... sanctified in Christ Jesus" (1 Cor 1:2). Scripture holds together what we are tempted to separate: the visible frailty of the church and its spiritual identity in Christ. The church is at once flawed and beloved, broken and being made whole.

This tension has always been central to Christian theology. Augustine spoke of the church as a *corpus permixtum* – a mixed body of saints and sinners, wheat and weeds.[1] The visible church is not identical to the invisible church, but the two are not separable in practice. This protects us from both idealism and despair. We are not surprised by sin in the church, nor do we mistake imperfection for failure. The church does not exist because it is flawless, but because it is forgiven. It is not a museum of righteousness; it is a workshop of redemption.

The Reformers made this distinction with pastoral clarity. Calvin wrote that wherever God's word is rightly preached and the sacraments rightly administered, there the church exists—even if it is full of weakness. He described the church as "the mother of all believers," through whom we are born, nourished, corrected, and formed.[2] The church, for Calvin, was not optional. It was the place where the gospel takes root, where discipleship unfolds, and where God meets His people.

This is what Screwtape despises. He wants believers to think of the church as a product to consume, not a people to belong to. He wants them to hop from congregation to congregation, measuring the music, critiquing the sermon, and resenting the members. He wants them to focus on the visible oddities and overlook

---

1. For Augustine's understanding of the church as *corpus permixtum*, see *On the Catechising of the Uninstructed* 1.17.26; 1.19.31, in NPNF 3:301–30.

2. Calvin, *Institutes*, 4.1.9.

The Church as a Battleground

the invisible grace. He wants them to dream of ideal community while withholding love from the real one. He wants to turn saints into cynics.

Imagine a man who grew up in the church. He remembers the potlucks, the baptisms, the campfire songs. But somewhere along the way, the warmth began to fade. He saw hypocrisy. He heard gossip. He was hurt by a leader he trusted. And so he withdrew—not all at once, but gradually. He still attends services, but with arms folded and heart guarded. He listens for mistakes in the sermon more than the voice of God. He notices awkward transitions in worship more than the grace behind the music. He sits among the saints, but with a critic's eye. The church, once his spiritual family, has become a religious performance he reviews each week. He hasn't abandoned the faith, but he no longer loves the bride. And in that subtle shift, Screwtape smiles. Because the goal was never apostasy—it was alienation. All Screwtape needed to do was exploit the real flaws of the church to blind him to its deeper glory.

But Scripture calls us to something more. The church is the body of Christ. We are not just saved from sin—we are saved into a family. This family is messy, but it is holy. It is imperfect, but it is beloved. And it is precisely in the grit of community—through confession, forgiveness, correction, and service—that God forms us. The local church is not the backdrop to discipleship. It is the context. It is the soil in which sanctification grows.

This is why staying in the church, week after week, is itself a spiritual discipline. It is easy to walk away when things get difficult. It is easy to harbor resentment or retreat into critique. But the call of Christ is to endure in love. To bear with one another. To forgive, as we have been forgiven. To show up. To serve. To sing beside the off-key and kneel beside the stubborn. This is not sentimentalism. It is spiritual war.

Discipleship is never private. It is deeply communal. The enemy would prefer we overlook this. He would rather us curate spiritual experiences online or in solitude. But real growth happens in covenantal community. It happens when we belong to people we wouldn't have chosen and stay through seasons we wouldn't have planned. Because it is in the awkward conversations, the shared burdens, the potlucks and the prayer chains, that Christ is present. The church is where he has promised to dwell.

That's why the devil fights so hard against it. The church proclaims the gospel, applies the sacraments, disciplines the heart, and sends forth the saints. It reminds us who we are and whose we are. It calls us out of isolation and into belonging. It trains us to see not just our preferences, but God's promises.

And so, to love the church is not naïve. It is Christlike. Christ gave himself for the church. He loves her as his bride. He is purifying her, even now, through his word and Spirit. To give up on the church is to give up on what Christ is doing. But to press in—to belong, to serve, to endure—is to participate in his work of redemption.

So commit. Not to an ideal church, but to a real one. Join a local body of believers—not because it is perfect, but because it is God's. Bring your gifts, your wounds, your questions, and your presence. Sing even when you don't feel like it. Serve even when it's unnoticed. Stay even when it's hard. Resist the consumer mindset that asks, "What am I getting from this?" and embrace the better question: "What is Christ forming in me through these people?" The church is not an accessory to your spiritual life—it is the place where your spiritual life is nurtured, challenged, and sustained. It is not always easy, but it is always worth it. Because in the mess and the beauty, in the weakness and the grace, this is where God is at work. This is where Christ is present. This is where you belong.

Let us then resist the demonic temptation to become consumers. Let us resist the drift into critique and isolation. Let us, instead, embrace the church as the battleground of grace. Let us love her as Christ does—not for what she is, but for what she is becoming.

The saints will sing on.

And Screwtape will rage in vain.

Chapter 8

Pain and Prosperity

"Now it may surprise you to learn that in His efforts to get permanent possession of a soul, He relies on the troughs even more than on the peaks; some of His special favourites have gone through longer and deeper troughs than anyone else." — *Screwtape*, Letter 8.

SUFFERING IS ONE OF the most ancient battlegrounds of spiritual warfare. It raises questions of God's goodness, God's presence, and God's power.1 The enemy seizes on these moments of weakness

---

1. These questions bring what has been called *theodicy*—the attempt to reconcile the existence of evil and suffering with the belief in a good, all-powerful, and all-knowing God. The term originates from the Greek words *theos* (God) and *dike* (justice), reflecting the quest to understand how divine justice coexists with human suffering. The challenge is profound: If God is good, why does he permit pain? If he is powerful, why doesn't he stop it? And if he is all-knowing, how can he allow it to continue? Theodicy seeks to reconcile these realities, affirming that God's goodness and sovereignty are not contradicted by the presence of suffering. Christian theologians, like Augustine and Aquinas, have argued that evil is not a created thing but a corruption of the good—an absence of good, much like darkness is an absence of light. Moreover, they contend that God permits suffering for reasons that often lie beyond human understanding, yet ultimately serve his purposes for redemption, growth, and the display of his glory. In Scripture, we see this most clearly in the story of Joseph—what his brothers intended for evil, God used for good (Gen 50:20)—and supremely at the cross, where the greatest act of injustice became the greatest act of redemption.

and pain not because suffering itself is evil, but because it is fertile ground for either despair or transformation.

In the *Screwtape Letters*, Lewis devotes significant attention to this dynamic. In Letter 8, Screwtape laments the fact that God often allows his people to undergo "troughs"—seasons of dryness, affliction, and sorrow—not because he has abandoned them, but because he intends to use those very trials for their deeper sanctification. "He really does want to fill the universe with a lot of loathsome little replicas of Himself," Screwtape sneers. And the way God does this is not through shielding his children from pain, but through shaping them by it.

Here we come face to face with one of the most challenging and essential truths of Christian discipleship: suffering is not the enemy of spiritual growth. It is often the means of it. And that is why, paradoxically, the very thing the enemy hopes will break us may be the very thing God uses to bless us.

THE AMBIGUITY OF SUFFERING IN HELL'S PLAYBOOK

Unlike popular caricatures of demonic temptation—where pain is always a weapon—Screwtape reveals a more complicated relationship with suffering. He cautions Wormwood against assuming that hardship automatically leads to spiritual ruin. On the contrary, if not carefully manipulated, suffering might actually drive the patient closer to God. He writes: "To us, a human is primarily food; our aim is the absorption of its will into ours, the increase of our own area of selfhood at its expense. But the obedience which the Enemy demands of men is quite a different thing. One must face the fact that all the talk about His love for men, and His service being perfect freedom, is not (as one would gladly believe) mere propaganda, but an appalling truth" (Letter 8).

Here Lewis reveals the fundamental contrast between Satan's kingdom and God's: the demonic purpose is to consume, to devour, to dehumanize. God's purpose, by contrast, is to sanctify,

PAIN AND PROSPERITY

to liberate, to make sons and daughters. And suffering, though a battleground, is often the place where that liberation begins.

Screwtape is disturbed by the paradox that when a Christian suffers and still chooses obedience—especially when all emotional and circumstantial encouragements are gone—the Enemy [God] gains a profound victory. In the fog of suffering, when the soul walks by faith and not by sight, hell is shaken.

THE DANGERS OF PROSPERITY

If Screwtape is nervous about suffering, he is perfectly at ease with prosperity. He knows that pain can awaken the soul, but comfort often lulls it to sleep. In Letter 13, he writes with sinister satisfaction: "Prosperity knits a man to the World. He feels that he is 'finding his place in it,' while really it is finding its place in him." This is a chilling line because it unveils the spiritual anesthetic of comfort. Prosperity, success, and ease do not need to argue against the gospel; they only need to make the gospel seem unnecessary. In seasons of plenty, the soul does not need to rage against God—it only needs to forget him. Spiritual lethargy rarely announces itself dramatically. It settles in quietly, like fog rolling over a city, obscuring the sharp contours of spiritual urgency and dulling the senses to the things of God. Comfort has a way of numbing the soul's appetite for transcendence. When everything appears secure, the desperation that drives us to our knees in times of trial evaporates. Heaven seems distant. The need for grace becomes less obvious. Screwtape delights in this numbing process because he understands that the soul that does not feel its need for God will not seek him.

This is one of Lewis's most urgent and prescient critiques of modern Western Christianity: the subtle, almost invisible danger of ease. In our Western post-Christian culture where suffering is generally rare and resources are abundant, the heart slowly reorients toward the world. When life is comfortable, the soul's reflex is not dependence but self-sufficiency. Prosperity creates the illusion of control. It whispers the lie that what you possess defines who you are, and what you achieve determines your worth. Screwtape leverages this illusion to great effect, dulling spiritual senses with the slow drip of self-satisfaction. It is not that the prosperous Christian disbelieves in God—it is that he forgets to need him. Security displaces dependence. Prayer becomes optional. Worship becomes routine. Gratitude grows thin. Eternity fades to a distant abstraction, while the immediate pleasures and goals of life become ultimate.

This numbing effect of prosperity is particularly dangerous because it is insidious. The soul rarely recognizes its drift toward complacency because the drift is gradual. Wealth, comfort, and success are not inherently evil, but they are spiritually volatile. Like fire, they have the power to warm or to destroy, depending on how they are handled. Scripture does not shy away from this warning. In Deuteronomy 8:11–14, God warns Israel not to forget him when they enter the Promised Land, eat their fill, and build fine houses. "Take care," he says, "lest your heart be lifted up, and you forget the Lord your God." Prosperity is a test, not of our capacity to enjoy good things, but of our ability to remain spiritually vigilant while enjoying them. Screwtape knows that comfort has a way of soothing the soul to sleep, of knitting the heart to the world so seamlessly that we do not even notice when our affections have been transferred from Christ to comfort.

The danger of prosperity is not simply materialism or greed, but the subtle reorientation of the heart away from heaven. Screwtape rejoices when the soul feels at home in Babylon, forgetting that it is called to Zion. This is why Jesus spoke so often of the dangers of wealth—not because it is inherently wicked, but because it is spiritually numbing. Comfort convinces us that we belong here, that our roots should grow deep in this world, that heaven can wait. But the gospel calls us to a different vision: we are pilgrims, sojourners, strangers in a foreign land. Prosperity tries to make us forget that. It lulls the soul into thinking that this life is all there is, that security is found in savings accounts, that happiness is found in possessions. Screwtape's strategy is simple but effective: make the Christian comfortable enough that he forgets he is at

Pain and Prosperity

war. A soul at ease is a soul unarmed. And that is exactly where Screwtape wants it.

By contrast, suffering interrupts this spiritual slumber. It breaks the illusion of control and exposes our weakness. Affliction reminds us that we are dust, that we are not in charge, and that our hope must be anchored in something far beyond this life. This is why suffering, though never easy, can be fruitful. It can refine our loves, redirect our desires, and reawaken our dependence on God. Paul speaks of affliction as a tool in God's hands—producing endurance, character, and hope (Rom 5:3–5). Screwtape knows this. He knows that suffering can backfire—because it has the potential to strip away idols and drive the soul deeper into the arms of grace.

Lewis himself would later write in *The Problem of Pain*: "God whispers to us in our pleasures, speaks in our conscience, but shouts in our pains: it is His megaphone to rouse a deaf world."[2] Pain is God's instrument of awakening—not because he delights in our suffering, but because he desires our sanctification. In *Screwtape*, that insight takes dramatic shape in the demon's frustration. Screwtape would prefer to keep the soul well-fed, well-entertained, and self-sufficient—undisturbed by mortality, untouched by need. But when suffering pierces the illusion, and the soul begins to cry out to God, he sees the danger: pain may be one of hell's tools, but it is also God's scalpel. It cuts with precision. It removes illusions. And, in the hands of the Great Physician, it can heal.

That is why prosperity must be approached with as much vigilance as adversity. The Christian life is not simply about weathering storms but remaining awake in sunshine. Ease must be met with gratitude, wealth with humility, comfort with dependence. Jesus warns of the choking thorns of worldly cares, riches, and pleasures (Luke 8:14)—not because they are inherently evil, but because they are spiritually numbing. Screwtape's strategy is to use those comforts to make the soul forget its need for God. But grace resists such forgetfulness. It teaches us, even in abundance, to hunger and thirst for righteousness. It teaches us to hold the world loosely, to live as pilgrims, and to remember that prosperity

---

2. Lewis, *The Problem of Pain*, 91.

is not proof of God's favor—nor is suffering proof of his absence. In both, he is present. In both, he is at work.

THE MAKING OF SAINTS IN THE FIRE

Perhaps the most profound moment comes in Letter 8, when Screwtape bitterly confesses his greatest fear: "Our cause is never more in danger than when a human, no longer desiring, but still intending to do our Enemy's will, looks round upon a universe from which every trace of Him seems to have vanished—and asks why he has been forsaken, and still obeys." This single sentence contains a wealth of theological insight. It is a portrait of spiritual maturity, forged not in seasons of clarity or abundance, but in the crucible of confusion and loss. It is faith distilled to its essence: obedience without reward, trust without sight.

This moment echoes the cry of Job in the ash heap, who, stripped of everything and unable to make sense of his suffering, declares, "Though he slay me, I will hope in him" (Job 13:15). It is the cry of Jesus in Gethsemane, sweating blood, praying, "Yet not my will, but yours be done" (Luke 22:42). It is the cry of the psalmist who, in the valley of the shadow of death, still whispers, "You are with me" (Ps 23:4). Lewis is pointing to something rare and precious: the kind of obedience that does not feed on emotional affirmation or circumstantial success, but rests solely on God's faithfulness. It is worship when the lights go out. It is loyalty in the dark.

This is not stoicism, nor is it blind resignation. It is the hard-won fruit of grace—a soul tested by fire and found clinging still to the promises of God. It is the spiritual steel of those who have faced the silence of heaven and still chosen to pray. These are the saints formed in the furnace—not in spite of the suffering, but through it. This is where sanctification and spiritual warfare converge. The devil's scheme is always the same: take pain and twist it into bitterness, cynicism, or despair. But God takes the very same pain and, through the Spirit, shapes it into holiness. The battlefield is interpretation—how we understand our trials. The weapon is trust—a refusal to allow suffering to speak the final word.

Mature discipleship is not marked by a pain-free life, but by perseverance through the pain. It is not measured by spiritual highs, but by spiritual endurance. The mature Christian is not the one who has all the answers, but the one who refuses to let go of Christ when there are no answers at all. Theologians have long recognized that the deepest work of sanctification happens not in times of prosperity, but in affliction. As Paul says, "Suffering produces endurance, and endurance produces character, and character produces hope" (Rom 5:3–4). This hope is not naïve optimism. It is forged in the fire. And that is why it cannot be shaken.

In seasons of suffering, the Christian does not deny the pain or pretend that all is well. The lament of the faithful is raw, honest, and full of tears. But lament is not faithlessness—it is faith speaking through grief. It is the cry of a child who still calls out to the Father. And because God is both sovereign over our suffering and present within it, the Christian can suffer without being undone. As David writes, "Even though I walk through the valley of the shadow of death, I will fear no evil, for you are with me" (Ps 23:4). That single phrase—*You are with me*—is the heart of Christian hope in affliction. Not that we will always be spared the valley, but that we will never walk it alone.

In these moments, the true nature of faith is revealed. Not as sentiment, but as allegiance. Not as ease, but as endurance. Lewis reminds us that suffering does not destroy genuine faith; it proves it. The kind of faith that endures suffering is not shallow or circumstantial—it is rooted in the unchanging character of God. It is a faith that has wrestled with the silence of God and still whispered "Amen." It is the quiet defiance of hell's strategy and the echo of heaven's perseverance. And for that reason, Screwtape is terrified of it. Because every saint who clings to God in suffering becomes a witness to the reality of grace, a living refutation of the lie that God is only good when life is easy.

This is why suffering, though bitter, can become sacred. Not because it is good in itself, but because in the hands of a sovereign and merciful God, it becomes the means of making us more like Christ. Hell trembles not at the Christian who prospers, but at the one who suffers well.

DEATH AND VICTORY

The patient's story ends not in defeat, but in death. And for Screwtape, death is a loss. Far from a moment of conquest, the man's death becomes the occasion for his entrance into glory. In the final letter, Screwtape's tone turns bitter, defeated, and resentful: "He got through so easily! No gradual misgivings, no doctor's sentence, no nursing home, no operating theatre, no false hopes of life; sheer, instantaneous liberation. One moment it seemed to be all our world; the scream of bombs, the fall of houses, the stink and taste of high explosive on the lips and in the lungs… and then silence and safety and the Enemy's country." What Screwtape describes with disgust is, from heaven's perspective, a triumph. The man's death in war—violent, abrupt, unromantic—was, in reality, the moment of his release into joy.

The demons had hoped to exploit this moment of terror. War, fear, and chaos are fertile ground for despair. But instead of weakening the man's faith, it revealed its strength. Instead of unraveling him, it carried him home. What for Screwtape is failure is, in God's eyes, victory. The soul that clung to God in the fog is now welcomed in the light. All the temptations, trials, and torments that seemed so strong have dissolved in the presence of glory. The irony is divine: what hell intended for evil, God used for eternal good. The cross and the crown remain inseparable in Lewis's vision of the Christian life—even in death.

Lewis paints death not as annihilation or terror, but as revelation. It is the unveiling. It is the moment when the soul passes from the veil of shadows into the brightness of God's kingdom. For those in Christ, death is not the end of life but the beginning of true life. As Paul writes, "To live is Christ, and to die is gain" (Phil 1:21). In death, the fog lifts. The longings are fulfilled. The weary soldier lays down his armor and hears the words, "Well done." No wonder Screwtape hates it—because death, for the redeemed, is not a defeat but a coronation.

What frustrates the demons most is not just that they lost. It's that they were outmatched by grace. The patient's suffering, loneliness, temptation, and death did not undo him. They purified him. He was refined, not consumed. The furnace they intended to destroy him only forged his faith. And now, he is beyond their reach. Their threats are silenced. Their accusations are overruled. He stands in the presence of the King, not because he earned it, but because he was kept. And this is the ultimate humiliation for hell—that grace is stronger than sin, that weakness endured in faith becomes glory, and that not even death can separate the soul from the love of God in Christ Jesus (Rom 8:38–39).

PASTORAL-THEOLOGICAL REFLECTION

Screwtape is not surprised by Christian joy in times of abundance. What he fears, what truly confounds the kingdom of darkness, is a Christian who still clings to Christ in the depths of pain. He mocks the peaks but trembles before the troughs. Why? Because he knows what many of us forget: that suffering, in the hands of God, is not a sign of absence but a means of sanctification.

Lewis's depiction of suffering is not speculative or sentimental. It is a dramatic rendering of theological truth rooted in Scripture and the tradition of the church. Suffering, according to Lewis, becomes the terrain where the soul is exposed, refined, and reclaimed. Screwtape sneers at the peaks of the Christian experience but panics when a believer walks through the valley and keeps praying. Because in the valley, God is doing deep work.

Picture a woman sitting in a hospital waiting room, her hands clenched tightly around a worn Bible. The test results were not good. Her future is uncertain. Her prayers are quiet now—less confident, more desperate. She doesn't have answers, only aches. And yet, she still prays. Still believes. Still whispers the name of Jesus. There's no emotional high, no visible miracle. Just a trembling soul refusing to let go. To the world, it looks like weakness. To

Screwtape, it looks like defeat. Because this is the kind of faith hell cannot explain—a faith that holds fast not when God feels near, but when he feels silent. A faith that survives not on experience, but on trust. Screwtape mocks joy when life is easy. But when a Christian clings to Christ in the dark, he trembles. Because suffering, in the hands of God, is never wasted. It is where idols die. Where pride is broken. Where the roots of faith grow deep.

Scripture does not shy away from this. From Joseph in prison to David in exile, from Job in ashes to Jesus in Gethsemane, suffering is where the soul is laid bare. Not because God is cruel, but because he is refining. And what Screwtape cannot stand—what shakes the very foundations of hell—is not a Christian who rejoices in blessing, but one who still worships in the valley. Because in that valley, the enemy's lies are shattered, and God's faithfulness is proven, not by comfort, but by communion.

Scripture teaches us to reframe suffering, not to romanticize it, but to redeem it. Paul writes that suffering produces endurance, character, and hope (Rom 5:3–4). James tells us to count it all joy (James 1:2–3). Peter says that trials refine our faith like gold (1 Pet 1:7). And Hebrews reminds us that discipline is the sign of God's fatherly love (Heb 12:6). In this vision, suffering is not divine punishment but divine pruning. It is the scalpel, not the sword.

This truth is not new. The early church bled with this conviction. Martyrs did not die because they had weak faith, but because they had resilient faith—a faith that counted the cost. Irenaeus emphasized that Christ's obedience in suffering was the means of uniting man with God. Tertullian called patience the defining Christian virtue. Augustine argued that suffering is not wasted because God brings good from evil. This was not abstract optimism. It was cross-shaped realism.[3]

The Reformers embraced this same truth. Calvin saw affliction not as a curse but as a classroom. The cross, he said, trains us in humility, hope, and eternal perspective. Suffering is not a detour from the Christian life; it is the path of discipleship. We

---

3. See Irenaeus, *Against Heresies* 5.21.1; Tertullian, *On Patience*, Chapter 1; Augustine, *Enchiridion*, Chapter 11 (Section 27).

are shaped not in comfort, but in cruciformity (the shape of the cross). And always, this shaping is governed by providence. Calvin insisted that no trial comes by chance, but by the wise hand of our Father.4 This is not fatalism—it is faith.

The *Heidelberg Catechism* captures it beautifully in the Q&A 1. In life and in death, we belong to Christ. Not a hair falls from our head without the will of our Father. And "all things must work together for my salvation." All things—even suffering. Especially suffering.

This is what the enemy dreads. He knows that pain, far from driving us from God, can drive us deeper into him. He knows that suffering scrapes away the illusion of self-reliance. It reveals the poverty of our idols. It breaks our pride. And in that breaking, grace enters. Suffering makes saints, not because we endure it well, but because Christ meets us in it.

The saints who suffer well are not triumphant by the world's standards. They are not polished or powerful. But they are tenacious. They cling to Christ when all else fails. They whisper prayers when the words barely come. They trust in the dark. And their endurance is not their achievement—it is the evidence that they are held.

Paul says that though our outer self is wasting away, our inner self is being renewed (2 Cor 4:16). The afflictions we face are preparing for us an eternal weight of glory (2 Cor 4:17). This is the paradox of the gospel: suffering is not just endured—it is redeemed. It is not just tolerated—it is transformed. The cross has turned the enemy's weapon into God's chisel.

And at the center of this hope is not a principle but a Person. Jesus Christ does not offer us escape from suffering. He offers us himself. He is the man of sorrows. He entered our pain. He bore our grief. He suffered for us and with us. And now, in him, our suffering is not meaningless. It is fellowship.

This is what Screwtape cannot comprehend. That a Christian might walk through agony and still sing. That a believer might lose

---

4. Calvin, *Institutes*, 3.8.1, 3.8.6, and 3.10.6. See also 1.17.1–11 for Calvin's doctrine of providence.

everything and still bless the name of the Lord. That a soul, bruised and weary, might still say, "Thy will be done."

Therefore, the victory of the gospel is not that we avoid suffering, but that suffering does not undo us. We are more than conquerors, Paul says, not because we escape hardship, but because Christ holds us through it (Rom 8:37). This is the brilliance of divine strategy: that the very things meant to destroy us become the means by which we are sanctified.

So hold fast. Do not interpret your pain as abandonment. Do not believe the lie that silence means absence. When the night grows long and the prayers feel unanswered, know that you are not alone. Christ has walked this path before you. And he walks it with you now. Commit yourself—not just in seasons of clarity, but especially in seasons of confusion. Cling to Christ when you don't understand. Worship when you don't feel it. Stay near when you want to flee. Because the valley is not void of God's presence—it is often where his grace runs deepest. And your perseverance in suffering is not weakness; it is holy defiance. It is a testimony that Christ is worthy—even here, even now.

Pain does not disprove God's love. It proves its depth. Prosperity may comfort us, but it rarely changes us. Pain, when met with grace, reshapes us. It makes us tender. It makes us dependent. It makes us long for the world to come. And this, ultimately, is why Screwtape fears the Christian who suffers well. Because that Christian becomes a signpost of glory. A testimony to the sustaining grace of God. A living witness that the gospel is true.

Let the furnace rage.

Grace burns brighter still.

Chapter 9

The Danger of Pride

"The Enemy [God] wants to bring the man to a state of mind in which he could design the best cathedral in the world, and know it to be the best, and rejoice in the fact, without being any more (or less) glad at having done it than he would be if it had been done by another." — *Screwtape*, Letter 14.

OF ALL THE WEAPONS in hell's arsenal, none is more corrosive to the Christian life than pride. It is the original sin of Satan—the desire not just to be like God, but to be above him (Isa 14:14). And it remains his most effective strategy, especially among those who are sincerely trying to grow in godliness.

Pride is dangerous not only because it is sinful, but because it is so easily disguised. It hides beneath virtues. It cloaks itself in achievement, humility, theology, even spiritual maturity. Lewis captures this with characteristic insight in Letters 13 and 14, where Screwtape urges Wormwood to subtly shift the patient's affections—not away from virtue, but toward a self-congratulatory delight in having achieved it.

This is the paradox of pride in the life of discipleship: it often grows in the very soil of our spiritual successes. The devil is pleased not just when we fail, but when we succeed and take credit for it. Because the goal is not just to stop our progress—it's to corrupt it.

Discipleship and Spiritual Warfare

PRIDE AS HELL'S PROTOTYPE

In Letter 14, Screwtape coaches Wormwood on how to distort his patient's growing humility. The patient has recently experienced a moment of genuine repentance, and with it, the first real traces of humility. But Screwtape urges his nephew not to panic. Humility, after all, can be turned into pride. If the man begins to notice that he has become humble—if he starts to feel pleased with his humility—then pride can begin to grow in the very soil of virtue. Screwtape writes: "Catch him at the moment when he is really poor in spirit and smuggle into his mind the gratifying reflection, 'By jove! I'm being humble,' and almost immediately pride—pride at his own humility—will appear." (Letter 14).

This is a diabolical brilliance: turning humility into vanity, gratitude into entitlement, faith into self-congratulation. Screwtape understands that pride does not always boast loudly. It can smile, bow politely, and still demand the center of the story.

Lewis is echoing his larger argument from *Mere Christianity*, where he writes, "Pride is spiritual cancer: it eats up the very possibility of love, or contentment, or even common sense."[1] What makes pride so deadly is not only that it separates us from others—it separates us from reality. The proud person is not merely self-centered. He is self-deceived. He cannot see clearly, because he sees everything through the distorted lens of self-importance.

WHEN VIRTUE BECOMES VICE

One of Lewis's most profound insights is that pride is not content to dwell in obvious sinners. It seeks out the virtuous. It creeps into the Christian life not by opposing goodness, but by corrupting it. Screwtape admits that God is most pleased when a man is able to do excellent work without needing to claim credit for it. This kind of humility—a self-forgetful joy in goodness—is dangerous to hell. The devils hate not just righteousness, but especially righteousness that is marked by quiet, grateful dependence on God.

1. Lewis, *Mere Christianity*, 112.

The Danger of Pride

Lewis illustrates how pride can corrupt even the most virtuous acts. Screwtape advises Wormwood to exploit the patient's religious practices by fostering a sense of superiority. This manipulation turns genuine humility into self-righteousness, as the individual begins to view his moral and theological correctness as personal achievements rather than gifts of grace. Screwtape further notes the danger of the patient becoming aware of his own humility, stating, "Your patient has become humble; have you drawn his attention to the fact?" (Letter 14). By doing so, the virtue of humility is tainted by pride, transforming it into a source of self-congratulation. Lewis's portrayal serves as a cautionary tale about the subtlety of pride and its ability to infiltrate and distort true virtue.

This is the temptation of the Pharisee in Jesus' parable: "God, I thank you that I am not like other men" (Luke 18:11). It is the sin of the elder brother in the parable of the prodigal son, who resents the celebration of grace because he believes he has earned something better (Luke 15:29–30). In both cases, the poison is the same: a deep sense of superiority disguised as devotion. What begins as faithfulness quietly shifts into performance. The heart ceases to marvel at mercy and begins to measure itself against others. Instead of drawing near to God with humility, the soul stands apart in pride. And yet, Scripture is clear: "God opposes the proud but gives grace to the humble" (James 4:6). True holiness never struts. It bows.

And this is what makes humility not only a virtue, but a battleground. For every act of obedience, there is a corresponding temptation to see oneself as better than others who have not done the same. Every hour spent in prayer can become an occasion for silent boasting. Every right belief can become a weapon of contempt. Lewis shows us that spiritual pride is not the opposite of godliness—it is its counterfeit. And it is all the more dangerous because it grows in the soil of spiritual effort. The antidote is not to abandon virtue, but to root it in grace—to see every good work as the fruit of God's mercy, not the proof of our merit. For the Christian, the goal is not to feel righteous, but to walk humbly with God

(Mic 6:8), always aware that the true measure of spiritual maturity is not how much we stand out, but how deeply we love.

THE ILLUSION OF CONTROL

Pride, as Lewis portrays it, is ultimately about control. It is the refusal to be dependent. It is the unwillingness to receive. Pride says, "I am the center," even if the words are never spoken aloud. It resists the idea that we are creatures—finite, fragile, and formed by grace. Pride is not content to be loved; it wants to be worthy of love. It is not satisfied with being saved; it wants to deserve salvation. And that is why it stands in direct opposition to the gospel, which begins not with human strength, but with human need.

In Letter 14, Screwtape confesses that real humility is deeply dangerous precisely because it acknowledges the truth of our creatureliness. Humility dismantles the illusion of control. It frees the soul from the exhausting burden of self-justification. It accepts the reality that we are not the source of our own goodness, not the center of the story, not the ones holding the world—or even our own lives—together. True humility is not the denial of one's gifts, but the refusal to make them the basis of one's identity. It is the freedom to live unselfconsciously in the presence of God.

This idea runs directly counter to Screwtape's strategy. He wants the patient to be forever turned inward: constantly analyzing his emotions, measuring his spiritual growth, and comparing himself to others. In this state of inner fixation, pride thrives. Because pride, at its core, is not mere arrogance—it is absorption. It is not always loud or boastful. Often, it is anxious, fragile, easily offended. It can dress itself in insecurity just as easily as in swagger. It turns the soul inward, even under the guise of spiritual self-examination. And the more we focus on ourselves—our performance, our image, our success—the less room we leave for God.

Lewis warns us here that self-obsession is not solved by self-loathing. It is solved by self-forgetfulness—a God-centered, others-oriented posture of life that finds joy in the glory of another. In this sense, humility is not merely a moral virtue; it is a form of spiritual liberation. It releases us from the tyranny of our own ego and reorients us toward worship. The truly humble person is not thinking constantly about how humble they are, or whether others recognize it. They are too busy delighting in the goodness of God, the beauty of others, and the wonder of grace. This is what Screwtape fears most—not the Christian who thinks poorly of himself, but the one who is finally free from needing to think about himself at all.

PRIDE IN DOCTRINE AND DEVOTION

One of Screwtape's sharpest and most sinister tactics is to nurture pride not in spite of religious identity, but through it. Let the patient become a devout churchgoer, a zealous student of Scripture, a careful theologian—and then let him begin to quietly look down on those who aren't. The danger is not in orthodoxy itself, but in what the heart does with it. The devil's goal is to turn love for truth into a badge of superiority, transforming discipleship into a private sense of spiritual entitlement. In this way, even the pursuit of holiness can be weaponized by pride.

In Letter 16, as mentioned before, Screwtape writes approvingly of Christians who become "connoisseurs of churches"—those who are more interested in evaluating the aesthetics, style, and theology of various congregations than in submitting to the hard work of belonging to a flawed community. And in Letter 23, he encourages the patient to develop religious opinions that are intellectually stimulating but practically disconnected from obedience. Let him become fascinated by the historical Jesus, enchanted by Greek words, obsessed with minor doctrinal debates—anything, so long as he stops asking whether he is loving his neighbor or submitting to Christ. Let theology become a distraction from transformation.

This is not, of course, a rejection of doctrine—far from it. Lewis loved doctrine, and so should we. Right belief is essential for right living. But Lewis also knew that theology is not an end in itself. It is a means to loving God more truly and living more

Discipleship and Spiritual Warfare

faithfully. When knowledge ceases to serve love, it begins to inflate the ego. As Paul warns in 1 Corinthians 8:1, "Knowledge puffs up, but love builds up." Theology, when rooted in humility, is a gift; when rooted in pride, it becomes a snare. Spiritual pride is more dangerous than ignorance, because it wears the mask of maturity. It hides in Bible studies, church councils, seminary classrooms, and even pulpits. And it whispers, "You're better because you know more."

When our theological clarity becomes a source of superiority rather than a means of worship, pride has taken root. When our prayer life becomes a performance for others—or even for ourselves—rather than communion with God, it has been corrupted. When our spiritual disciplines become points of comparison rather than postures of dependence, we have crossed into the territory Screwtape prefers. It is possible to read Scripture daily and miss the heart of the Father. It is possible to defend doctrine fiercely while lacking love. And it is possible to appear spiritually disciplined while being spiritually detached. This is the great inversion of pride: it can make even holiness into a pedestal.

What Screwtape delights in most is not the heretic, but the orthodox man who uses his orthodoxy to elevate himself. Not the irreligious, but the deeply religious person who thinks his religion makes him superior. The enemy wants us to know the truth. Screwtape wants us to use the truth to serve the self. And so the antidote is not to abandon doctrine or devotion, but to anchor them in grace. To remember that we are not saved by our accuracy, our consistency, or our zeal—but by the mercy of God. Every insight into truth should make us bow lower. Every discipline should deepen our love. Every act of worship should end in wonder, not self-congratulation. Because the closer we draw to God, the more we see: He alone is holy, and all we have is gift.

HUMILITY AS RESISTANCE

Though Screwtape loathes humility, he cannot deny its power. He knows that a truly humble Christian—a person who is no longer

The Danger of Pride

obsessed with self-image, who is content to serve unnoticed, who rejoices in the good even when it's done by others—is a threat to hell's designs. Humility disarms the enemy precisely because it disarms the ego. It refuses to play by the rules of pride, comparison, and self-promotion. It sees through the devil's game and refuses to participate.

This is because humility brings freedom. It liberates the soul from the tyranny of reputation. It quiets the need for constant affirmation. It silences the lie that we are what others think of us. And it opens the heart to grace. A humble person is teachable, because they know they need help. They are forgiving, because they know how much they've been forgiven. They are generous with honor, because they don't feel threatened by the success of others. In a world obsessed with visibility, the humble are content to live in the background, trusting that God sees, and that is enough.

And Screwtape prefers the proud Christian, not because such a person is overtly sinful, but because he is manipulable. He is defensive. He is self-important. He is easily offended and quick to judge. Every slight becomes a wound and every compliment becomes a snare. Pride makes the soul reactive, insecure, and brittle. But the humble Christian is stable, grounded, unshaken. He cannot be flattered and is hard to provoke. He has no illusions about his own greatness, and so he is not afraid to be wrong. He lives in the truth and welcomes correction. He listens more than he speaks, prays more than he performs, and loves without needing to be noticed.

And that, Lewis suggests, is what makes him most like Christ. For Christ, though he was in the form of God, did not count equality with God a thing to be grasped, but humbled himself—taking the form of a servant, becoming obedient even to the point of death (Phil 2:6-8). True humility is not weakness; it is divine strength under restraint. It is the posture of heaven. And when a Christian walks in that humility, he becomes a living contradiction to the kingdom of darkness—a quiet, joyful rebellion against the tyranny of self. No wonder Screwtape fears it. For humility, once formed in the soul, becomes one of the surest signs that God's grace is winning.

PASTORAL-THEOLOGICAL REFLECTION

Lewis paints pride not simply as an individual sin but as the primal distortion at the heart of all sin. His depiction is in line with the classical Christian consensus: that pride is the root from which all vices grow. In *The City of God*, Augustine writes, "Pride is the beginning of sin."2 It was pride that caused the fall of Lucifer (Isa 14:13–14), pride that enticed Adam and Eve to grasp at autonomy (Gen 3:5–6), and pride that continues to drive the human impulse to dethrone God and enthrone the self.

The biblical witness treats pride as the antithesis of grace. "God opposes the proud but gives grace to the humble" (James 4:6; see also 1 Pet 5:5). Proverbs declares, "Pride goes before destruction, and a haughty spirit before a fall" (Prov 16:18). In Scripture, pride is not a flaw in the margins of the soul—it is a frontal assault against God. It is the root of folly, idolatry, and relational rupture. It blinds, isolates, and calcifies the heart against repentance and love.

Theologically, pride is not merely a behavioral vice; it is a misjudgment of reality. It distorts our anthropology (our vision of man) and our theology (our vision of God). It is the illusion of independence—the refusal to acknowledge creatureliness and dependence upon God. John Calvin insists, "Man never achieves a clear knowledge of himself unless he has first looked upon God's face."3 In other words, self-awareness is impossible apart from God-awareness. Pride thrives in forgetfulness of God.

Picture a man who has done everything right—at least in his own eyes. He's built a respectable life, earned a good reputation, and is known in the church as a man of conviction. He reads theology, defends doctrine, and serves the church. But slowly, almost

---

2. Augustine, *City of God*, 12.6.
3. Calvin, *Institutes*, 1.1.2.

imperceptibly, something shifts. He no longer seeks correction. He avoids vulnerability. He talks about God, but rarely to God. He offers counsel but cannot receive it. What began as faithfulness has hardened into self-assurance. Beneath the surface, he has begun to believe a lie: that he stands above the need for grace. He has become unteachable, unreachable, closed off. And that is precisely where pride does its deadliest work—not in overt rebellion, but in subtle self-reliance. Screwtape could not be more pleased. Because pride does not need to break a man openly; it only needs to convince him that he no longer needs a Savior.

Lewis understands this well. He shows that pride is not always loud or self-aggrandizing. Sometimes it masquerades as spiritual maturity or intellectual clarity. It creeps into piety, discipleship, orthodoxy—even humility itself. As Augustine said, pride is "the love of one's own excellence."4 This is why Screwtape is so pleased when his patient becomes proud of being humble. Nothing pleases hell more than virtue turned to vanity.

The early church fathers viewed pride as the first and deadliest sin because it attacks the very structure of grace. Some would call identify pride as "the queen of sins," the root from which all others descend.5 In his *Ladder of Divine Ascent*, John Climacus famously placed humility at the top of the ladder of spiritual

---

4. Augustine, *On Nature and Grace*, 33.29. See also Augustine, *City of God*, 12.6.

5. Pride has long been considered the foremost of all sins by many Church Fathers. St. Augustine describes pride as the very "origin of our evil will," citing that "pride is the beginning of sin" (*City of God*, 14.13). St. Gregory the Great explicitly calls pride the "queen of sins" and explains that "when pride, the queen of sins, has fully possessed a conquered heart, she surrenders it immediately to seven principal sins, as if to some of her generals, to lay it waste" (*Moralia in Job*, 31.45). John Cassian similarly emphasizes its supreme danger, observing that "after His victory over gluttony, [Satan] did not venture to tempt Him to fornication, but passed on...to pride, by which he knew that those who are perfect and have overcome all other sins, can be affected" (*Conference* 5.13). Thomas Aquinas, reflecting on Gregory's teachings, reiterates that "Gregory, however, reckons pride to be the queen of all the vices" (*Summa Theologica*, II-II, Q. 132, Art. 4).

growth and pride at the bottom, describing humility as "a mysterious force in the soul" known only through experience.6

Humility, in contrast, is not a denial of dignity but a recognition of dependence. It is grounded in truth—the truth of God's greatness and our need for him. In Luke 18, the tax collector prays simply, "God, be merciful to me, a sinner" (Luke 18:13). Jesus calls this man, not the self-congratulatory Pharisee, justified. Philippians 2:6-8 shows that Christ, though truly God, humbled himself to the point of death. Humility is the mind of Christ. To be humble, then, is not to think less of oneself, but to think of oneself rightly before God.

The Reformers kept this understanding central. Luther viewed the entire Christian life as one of repentance. The first of his 95 Theses reads: "When our Lord and Master Jesus Christ said 'Repent,' he willed the entire life of believers to be one of repentance." Repentance, of course, presupposes humility. And spiritual growth is directly proportional to one's awareness of need and capacity to receive grace.

This is why the proud Christian is a theological contradiction. He may appear morally upright and doctrinally sound, but pride turns truth into a weapon and virtue into a mirror. John Owen said that "Rank, honor, domination, and pride do not make theologians."7 Pride bends every good thing inward. It cannot rejoice in others, submit to correction, or receive unmerited grace. And this, as Lewis shows, is precisely why Screwtape loves it.

Pride not only halts sanctification—it reverses it. The proud become unteachable. The Spirit is grieved. The soul hardens. In contrast, the humble soul becomes receptive to the Spirit's work. As Isaiah declares, "I dwell in the high and holy place, and also with him who is of a contrite and lowly spirit" (Isa 57:15). Humility, then, is not optional. It is the condition for communion with God. It is the soil in which all other virtues grow—love, patience, joy, and faith. Where pride isolates, humility integrates. It opens

---

6. Climacus, *The Ladder of Divine Ascent*, 25.2.
7. John Owen, *Biblical Theology*, xxvi.

the self to others and to God. And in that openness, transformation begins.

So how do we resist pride in the life of discipleship? We start by fixing our eyes on Christ. Pride shrinks in the presence of his glory. When we gaze upon the crucified and risen Lord, we see both the depth of our need and the height of his grace. We remember that everything we have is a gift. We repent not just of our sins, but of our pride in our virtues. We resist pride through confession—regular, honest, corporate. We resist it through service—doing unseen work with no applause. We resist it through community—inviting correction, listening to the wisdom of others, refusing to isolate ourselves in superiority. And above all, we resist pride by embracing joy. Not the joy of self-achievement, but the joy of knowing we are loved apart from our performance. The joy of grace. This is the joy that Screwtape cannot counterfeit. Because it is rooted not in us, but in Christ.

The greatest danger of pride is not that it makes us feel strong—but that it blinds us to our weakness. It blocks the channels of grace by convincing us we have no need. It makes love impossible because it cannot bear to be lesser. It turns truth into self-justification and community into competition. It builds identity on illusion and hides the soul in shadow. But humility is the threshold of the kingdom. It is the gateway to healing and the ground of joy. The humble person is not insecure—he is secure enough to forget himself. He is free to listen, to laugh, to serve, to repent. He knows his need, and so he rejoices in grace.

Lewis reminds us that pride is the sin most admired in the world and least recognized in ourselves. But the truly humble person is the freest. He can enjoy beauty, truth, and goodness—even when they are found in others. He can laugh at his mistakes. He can be corrected without crumbling. He can serve without bitterness and receive without pride. And that kind of soul is dangerous to the enemy. Because that kind of soul is becoming like Christ. Screwtape trembles when a soul stops looking at itself and starts looking to Jesus.

So humble yourself. Not in a false performance of humility, but in true, trembling awareness of your need for grace. Return again to the foot of the cross, where pride dies and love lives. Ask God to search your heart, to reveal where self-reliance has taken root. Let go of the need to be impressive. Resist the urge to control, to justify, to exalt yourself. Confess—not just your failures, but your pride in pretending you had none. And when you do, you will find that the God who opposes the proud does not crush the humble—he lifts them. He draws near. He gives grace. Because the way up in the kingdom of God is always down. And the moment we stop trying to be strong is the moment we are finally free to be formed.

Let the proud parade.

The humble will inherit the earth.

Chapter 10

The Kingdom and the World

> "Let him begin by treating the Patriotism or the Pacifism as a part of his religion. Then let him, under the influence of partisan spirit, come to regard it as the most important part. Then quietly and gradually nurse him on to the stage at which the religion becomes merely part of the 'cause.'" — *Screwtape*, Letter 7.

ONE OF THE ENEMY'S most subtle strategies is not to deny the Christian faith but to dilute it. Rather than destroy discipleship outright, Screwtape prefers to redirect it—to shift the believer's center of gravity from Christ to culture, from the eternal to the political, from the gospel to ideology. This is spiritual warfare not by confrontation, but by confusion.

Lewis devotes Letter 7 and 23 to this very tactic. Screwtape encourages Wormwood to inflame the patient's political opinions—whether conservative or progressive, it doesn't matter—so long as the patient begins to see his political cause as the essence of his religion. "The thing to do," Screwtape advises, "is to get a man at first to value social justice as a thing which the Enemy demands, and then work him on to the stage at which he values Christianity because it may produce social justice." (Letter 23). The goal is reversal. Not Jesus as Lord over all of life, but life repurposed in service of worldly loyalties.

Discipleship and Spiritual Warfare

This chapter explores the spiritual battleground of the mind. Not merely intellectual assent, but worldview allegiance. Who shapes the way we think? What defines what we value? What kingdom do we truly belong to? In short: how is the Christian mind formed—and what forces seek to deform it?

HOW TO POLITICIZE A SOUL

In Letter 7, Lewis immerses the reader into one of the defining moral and spiritual crises of the twentieth century: the Second World War. This setting is far from incidental. Lewis writes during a period when nationalism, militarism, and ideological tribalism were not mere abstractions but brutal, lived realities. Yet, even in such a turbulent time, Lewis warns that political engagement itself is not the inherent threat to Christian witness—it is the misalignment of allegiances.

Screwtape, the senior demon, eagerly instructs Wormwood to "fix the patient on politics." The specific party or ideology is inconsequential; what matters is the displacement of faith. The objective is to make Christianity subservient to political aims, reducing it to a mere instrument for achieving secular ends. Screwtape explains this tactic bluntly: "Once you have made the World an end, and faith a means, you have almost won your man. And it makes very little difference what kind of worldly end he is pursuing" (Letter 7).

Lewis's warning is profound in its simplicity: when faith is subordinated to political ideology, it ceases to function as a transcendent guide and instead becomes a weaponized tool for worldly ambition. This manipulation is not restricted to any single political side—a fact Screwtape gleefully acknowledges. What matters is not the content of the ideology, but its ability to displace the primacy of Christ.

In Letter 23, Screwtape elaborates on the tactic of redirecting Christian faith toward political or social ends, hollowing out its true essence. The method is insidious: begin with a cause the believer genuinely values—peace, justice, national security, or religious freedom. Then, subtly suggest that this cause is not merely important but central to the gospel itself. From there, persuade him that his perspective on the matter is the only faithful Christian stance. Finally, lead him to believe that those who disagree are not just mistaken but fundamentally flawed—ignorant, immoral, or even unfaithful.

At this stage, the church morphs into a political tribe, Scripture becomes a mere prop, and Christ is reduced to a mascot for ideology. Screwtape captures the danger precisely: "Let him begin by treating the Patriotism or the Pacifism as a part of his religion. Then let him, under the influence of partisan spirit, come to regard it as the most important part. Then quietly and gradually nurse him on to the stage at which the religion becomes merely part of the 'cause,' in which Christianity is valued chiefly because of the excellent arguments it can produce in favour of the British war effort or of Pacifism."

What Screwtape knows—and what many postmodern believers forget—is that political idolatry often wears the clothes of moral passion. When Christians allow partisanship to dictate discipleship, they may still use Christian language, but their allegiance has shifted. They are being discipled more by cable news than by the word of God. Their liturgy is talk radio. Their eschatology is election cycles. Their church is a voting bloc. The cross becomes a symbol of identity, not a call to die.

This is precisely what Screwtape aims to do. He wants the patient to adopt a kind of "Christianity and…" religion. Christianity and politics. Christianity and nationalism. Christianity and progressivism. The content of the "and" doesn't matter—the point is that it becomes the controlling center. The gospel becomes a servant, not the sovereign. Screwtape doesn't care whether the Christian becomes a pacifist or a patriot—only that his identity becomes wrapped up in one of them. When Christianity becomes a tool of ideology, it ceases to be salt and light. It becomes flavorless. Or worse—it becomes fuel.

Discipleship and Spiritual Warfare

THE CLOUD OF "SPIRITUAL" CONFUSION

If political distortion is one ditch, spiritual vagueness is another. And Screwtape is equally pleased with both. If Wormwood cannot radicalize his patient's politics, he can dilute his theology. Let the patient become vague. Let him grow increasingly "spiritual," increasingly abstract, increasingly fascinated with mystical experiences—while avoiding doctrinal clarity, moral accountability, and biblical substance. Let his faith become a fog, full of feeling but empty of foundation. Let him talk endlessly about "light" and "love" and "connection," but never about the cross, sin, or truth.

Lewis anticipates here the postmodern drift into religious indifference—what we now call *Moralistic Therapeutic Deism*.[1] In this form of temptation, the Christian faith is reduced to a benign sentimentality. God becomes a vague cosmic therapist: benevolent, affirming, and distant. He wants us to be kind, to feel good, and to avoid suffering—but not to repent, submit, or die to self. Sin is rebranded as brokenness, judgment is dismissed as unloving, and doctrine is seen as arrogant or irrelevant. Church becomes optional, Scripture becomes inspirational, and Jesus becomes a sage instead of a Savior. The result is a form of Christianity that retains its vocabulary but loses its voice.

The brilliance of this temptation lies in its comfort. This kind of "faith" costs nothing. It demands no repentance. It never offends, never confronts, never transforms. It blends seamlessly into a pluralistic society, offering vague hope without holy fear. But Screwtape knows what it lacks: power. Vague spirituality cannot cast out demons. It cannot raise the dead. It cannot sustain a soul through the valley of suffering or anchor a life in the face of death. It cannot birth courage, cultivate holiness, or endure persecution. It is a mist that evaporates when the heat of trial comes. And worst of all, it poses no threat to hell.

Lewis's answer to this drift is not rigidity or sectarian pride. It is *Mere Christianity*—not Christianity stripped of depth, but

---

1. See chapter 5 of my book *Discipleship in a Post-Christian Age* (2025) for a more detailed account of Moralistic Therapeutic Deism.

Christianity rooted in essentials: anchored in the person of Jesus Christ, rooted in the word of God, lived in communion with the triune God, and expressed in personal and communal obedience. In a world drifting toward religious haze, the call is not to build higher fences but to recover the clarity of gospel light. The vague Christian mind is a fog that needs the burning light of truth. Only a faith that is grounded in Christ—crucified, risen, and reigning—can stand firm in the cultural storm. And only such faith can resist Screwtape's schemes.

ALLEGIANCE TO THE KINGDOM OF CHRIST

What both politicized religion and diluted spirituality have in common is a failure of formation. They may appear opposed—one loud and dogmatic, the other vague and indifferent—but beneath the surface, both reveal a heart unshaped by the gospel. In both cases, the Christian mind is conformed to the spirit of the age. The imagination is captivated not by Christ, but by cultural idols. Instead of being renewed by the word of God, the soul is subtly discipled by the world—through news cycles, algorithms, ideologies, and slogans. Instead of living under the lordship of Jesus, the believer bows to the gods of tribe, politics, comfort, identity, or self-expression—whether clothed in a flag or wrapped in mysticism.

But Jesus does not call his people to a middle ground. He calls them to himself. The gospel is not merely a message of personal forgiveness—it is a royal announcement. It is the declaration that a new kingdom has arrived, and its king is Christ. To believe the gospel is to be transferred from the domain of darkness into the kingdom of the beloved Son (Col 1:13). It is to submit to a new authority, a new ethic, a new center of gravity. "My kingdom is not of this world," Jesus said to Pilate (John 18:36). And yet, his kingdom is decisively in the world—a subversive, transforming presence that claims every inch of our lives: our politics, our work, our economics, our habits, our relationships, our sexuality, our art, our desires. Nothing is untouched by his reign.

This is why the renewal of the Christian mind is not optional—it is essential. "Do not be conformed to this world," Paul writes, "but be transformed by the renewal of your mind" (Rom 12:2). This is not a call to mere intellectualism. It is a call to discipleship that begins in the imagination and extends to action. The renewed mind sees with gospel clarity. It discerns false narratives. It resists the formation of cultural liturgies. It is not satisfied with being "spiritual" or "moral" or "informed"—it longs to be holy, Christlike, and wise. The Christian mind is not shaped passively. It must be trained, tested, and tuned to the truth. And that training takes place in the word, among the church, and through daily submission to Christ's lordship.

A Christian mind is a mind that sees the world through the lens of redemption. It sees politics not as a means of power, but as a platform for neighbor love and justice. It sees work not as a burden or idol, but as vocation. It sees suffering not as meaningless pain, but as the soil of sanctification and a fellowship with Christ (Phil 3:10). It sees human dignity as grounded in the image of God, not in utility or performance. It sees beauty and truth not as subjective preferences, but as echoes of the Creator's glory. Most of all, it sees Christ—not as an accessory to life, but as its center. He is the Alpha and the Omega, the source and the goal. The kingdom of Christ is not one compartment of life—it is the framework through which all of life is reimagined. And the more the Christian mind is formed by that kingdom, the less power Screwtape and his schemes will have.

LIVING WITH DISCERNMENT

In Letter 7, Screwtape vents his frustration that the patient has joined a church that is simply "mere Christian." This, for Screwtape, is intolerable. Such a church lacks the distortions of ideology or the vanity of vague sentiment. It does not cater to trends, factions, or fads. It does not exist to promote a political platform or a spiritual brand. It is focused on Christ—on the ancient gospel, the apostolic faith, the truth once for all delivered to the saints. And for that reason, it is dangerous. Screwtape much prefers a church that has been subtly hijacked—by activism, emotionalism, nationalism, or intellectualism. But a church centered on Christ alone is an existential threat to hell.

The challenge for Christians today is no different. We must resist being co-opted by culture, even as we live within it. We are not called to isolation or indifference, but to discernment. Withdrawal is not faithfulness, but neither is compromise. The Christian's task is to be present without being absorbed, engaged without being defined by the age. As Paul wrote to the Philippians, we are to "shine as lights in the world, holding fast to the word of life" (Phil 2:15-16). This requires a mind formed not by reaction to headlines, but by revelation from Scripture. We must refuse to give our hearts to passing kingdoms when we belong to an unshakable one (Heb 12:28).

This is what Lewis meant when he famously wrote, "Aim at heaven and you will get earth 'thrown in': aim at earth and you will get neither."[2] The Christian life is not lived by drifting with the current, but by swimming upstream—toward a kingdom that is not of this world, yet deeply in it. To aim at heaven is not to escape earthly concerns but to approach them with eternal clarity. It is to live under the lordship of Christ in every sphere—our thoughts, our politics, our relationships, our vocations. It is to love God supremely and our neighbor rightly, not with sentimentality, but with wisdom shaped by the gospel. A heavenly-minded Christian is the most earthly-useful kind of person—not because they ignore the world, but because they understand its true story.

Screwtape's nightmare is not the Christian who is noisy and distracted, nor the one who is consumed with spiritual novelty or cultural rage. His nightmare is the Christian who sees clearly, loves deeply, thinks biblically, and lives quietly for the kingdom. That Christian cannot be easily manipulated. He is not impressed by power, nor moved by fear. She is not consumed with image or influence, but with faithfulness and fruit. That Christian is rooted in truth and animated by grace. That Christian has learned to

---

2. Lewis, *Mere Christianity*, 135.

resist the world not with withdrawal, but with wisdom. And in doing so, that Christian becomes truly human—restored, free, and fully alive in Christ. That Christian, Screwtape knows, is becoming dangerous.

PASTORAL-THEOLOGICAL REFLECTION

At the heart of Screwtape's strategy is not simply the corruption of behavior but the deformation of the Christian imagination. If Screwtape can form the mind, the hands and heart will follow. This is no minor tactic. It is a direct assault on the image of God, which includes the human capacity for reason, reflection, and worship. And so, the true battleground is epistemological before it is ethical—a war over how we see, think, and understand the world. In biblical terms, the call to discipleship is a call to think differently.

The transformation of the mind that Paul mentions in Romans 12:2 is not a mental exercise alone; it is an act of allegiance. It is a renunciation of worldly narratives and the embrace of God's story as the true story of the world.

Lewis understood that every Christian is being formed by something. The question is not whether we are being discipled, but by whom. And the enemy's goal is to ensure that formation happens quietly, imperceptibly, through subtle distortions that eventually yield profound disloyalties. Politicized religion and vague spiritualism are among his favorites because they are socially acceptable, even celebrated, while emptying the faith of its cross-bearing core.

The danger of politicized religion is not merely division, but idolatry. It baptizes temporal ideologies in eternal language and binds the name of Christ to the slogans of Caesar. It reshapes our affections and fears around the success or failure of worldly powers, rendering the eternal kingdom of God as a secondary concern. And vague spiritualism—that formless, harmless religiosity detached from Scripture—is just as damaging. It offers sentiment without substance, a god made in our image, incapable of saving or sanctifying. Together, these distortions sever the mind from truth and the heart from grace.

Imagine a Christian who begins each day not with Scripture or prayer, but with hours of cable news, social media feeds, and cultural commentary. Over time, without realizing it, their hopes rise and fall with election cycles, and their language sounds more like a political pundit than a disciple of Christ. They speak passionately about national decline but grow silent when asked about the fruits of the Spirit. Another Christian, longing for peace in a chaotic world, turns to a vague spirituality of self-care and cosmic vibes. Their bookshelf is full of devotionals about inner light, but the cross is strangely absent. Both feel spiritually alive, but neither is being formed by the gospel. This is how the enemy works—not through blatant rejection of the faith, but through slow, subtle shifts in loyalty. Formation is always happening. The only question is whether we are being shaped by Christ or by a counterfeit.

Practically speaking, this means we must regularly examine whether our faith is centered on Christ or subtly co-opted by cultural agendas. Both the political right and left are vulnerable to this distortion. On the right, Christianity can become a vehicle for cultural preservation, national identity, or moral superiority. On the left, it can morph into a tool for personal expression, social progress, or therapeutic validation. In both cases, faith is no longer about Christ but about what He can do to support our cause. The danger isn't always obvious—it often comes through passion for justice, truth, or righteousness, but slowly replaces the gospel with a functional idol. The irony is that we may feel spiritually energized and deeply convicted while, in reality, drifting into a Christless activism or self-righteous complacency. That's why we need the regular disciplines of Scripture, worship, confession, and community—to re-center our hearts on Jesus. Christianity is not a means to another end; it is the end. Any version of faith that makes Christ secondary—no matter how noble the cause—is a counterfeit.

The devil knows how easily the Christian mind can be distracted from Christ. All he needs is a cause or a feeling to take center stage. The great irony is that the Christian might believe he is growing in maturity while, in fact, drifting into irrelevance. When Christianity becomes a means to another end—whether cultural dominance or personal fulfillment—it ceases to be Christianity. It becomes a tool of the self rather than the call to deny the self. The renewal of the Christian mind, then, is not a retreat into intellectualism but an advance into holiness. It is a reformation of perception. It is learning to see the world as God sees it: through the lens of creation, fall, redemption, and consummation. It is understanding that truth is not an abstract idea but a person—Jesus Christ, the word made flesh. And it is through abiding in him that the mind is renewed.

Worship is where this renewal begins. In the ordinary rhythm of word and sacrament, of praise and confession, our disordered loves are reordered. The liturgy trains the mind by training the heart. It speaks the truth again and again until it sinks beneath the surface of awareness. In worship, we are reminded of who God is, who we are, and what story we are in. And this liturgical formation becomes the foundation for all other discernment.

But this renewal also demands community. Christian thinking is not the work of solitary geniuses but of a Spirit-filled body. The church is where young minds are catechized, where old minds are sharpened, and where all minds are humbled. It is where we are corrected, instructed, and encouraged. To form a Christian mind is to form Christian friendships—with people who help us think not only clearly, but faithfully.

None of this is easy in an age of distraction and polarization. But it is essential. Because the Christian mind is not merely a mind with Christian opinions. It is a mind that processes the world through the cross and resurrection. It is a mind that does not flinch in the face of suffering or become intoxicated with power. It is a mind that refuses to be discipled by headlines and algorithms, choosing instead the slow, daily formation of Scripture and prayer.

Ultimately, this is a question of allegiance. To whom does the mind belong? Who sets the terms of truth, beauty, and goodness? Who defines what it means to be human, to be free, to be fulfilled? Screwtape wants the patient to believe these are neutral questions—matters of preference. But the gospel teaches otherwise. We are creatures. We were made for God. And to be truly human is to know and love him with heart, soul, strength, and mind.

Therefore, in an age marked by cultural confusion and spiritual compromise, the disciple of Christ is called not to retreat, but to stand firm—rooted, not reactive. We are not commanded to escape the world, but to be transformed within it. The line between faithfulness and conformity is often subtle, but the stakes are anything but small. The church today is not only tempted by overt worldliness but by subtler forms of drift: politicized religion that baptizes partisan agendas, and vague spirituality that abandons theological clarity for therapeutic slogans. But discipleship requires more. It requires consecration—not to a party or ideology, but to Christ and His kingdom.

This consecration begins in the mind. The renewal of the mind is not a call to academic elitism; it is a spiritual imperative. To "be transformed by the renewal of your mind" (Rom 12:2) is to think with gospel-formed clarity, to see the world through the lens of the cross and resurrection. It is to bring every thought captive to Christ (2 Cor 10:5)—not as a heavy burden, but as liberation from the tyranny of self and the illusions of the age. Discipleship that neglects the mind leaves the church vulnerable to false gospels—whether they come wrapped in political banners or spiritual sentimentality.

To follow Jesus, then, is to think with eternity in view. It is to judge success, power, identity, and truth not by the metrics of the moment but by the measure of the kingdom. It is to love what Christ loves, to hate what he hates, and to trust what he has promised—even when it puts us out of step with the world. The Christian mind is not conformed to the patterns of this age but conformed to Christ himself, shaped by Scripture, grounded in truth, and alive to the Spirit's renewing power.

The danger is not merely moral failure. The deeper danger is spiritual irrelevance—the kind that masquerades as faithfulness while avoiding real surrender. The enemy is content when Christians appear active but remain untransformed. When they speak of justice but resist holiness. When they profess Christ but refuse to be corrected by his word. In such cases, the devil need not provoke open rebellion; he only needs to feed our self-assurance. That is how pride, distraction, and tribal loyalties displace the kingdom.

The formation of the Christian mind, then, is not optional—it is essential. We become what we contemplate. And in a world that relentlessly shapes our thinking through headlines, algorithms, and ideological scripts, the call to think Christianly is a matter of survival. It means seeing reality as God sees it, reasoning in light of Scripture, and imagining our lives within the greater story of redemption. Discipleship is not just about doing what Jesus says; it is about learning to see the world as Jesus sees it. That is the battleground of the mind—and the beginning of true transformation.

Chapter 11

The Christian Journey

"He is now safe in our Enemy's house... You have let a soul slip through your fingers." — *Screwtape,* Letter 31.

AT THE END OF the *Screwtape Letters*, the battle is over. Not with fire or spectacle, but with quiet finality. The patient dies. And in the instant of death—the moment Screwtape dreads most—the patient is received into the presence of God. "He got through so easily!" Screwtape snarls. The demons have lost. The soul they worked so tirelessly to erode has been kept. Not by his own strength, but by the faithfulness of the One who called him.

This is the end of the patient's journey. But it is also the goal of every Christian life: to persevere. To reach the finish line—not unscarred, but still in the race. And to be welcomed, not because we were strong, but because we were his. Perseverance is the doctrine of divine faithfulness. It is not about never falling. It is about never being forsaken. It is the comforting truth that the Christian is held—through every season, every sin, every sorrow—by a grace that refuses to let go.

THE ARC OF THE PATIENT'S SOUL

The patient's spiritual journey is not linear. It is uneven, full of ups and downs, and deeply human. His conversion, which occurs quietly between Letters 1 and 2, is not the end of the story but the beginning of a lifelong tug-of-war for his soul. He attends church but finds the other congregants awkward and unimpressive. He begins to pray, but his mind drifts. He seeks meaning but is easily drawn into superficial friendships and worldly distractions. He sins and repents. He makes promises and breaks them. His spiritual life is not marked by triumphal ascent but by repeated stumbles—and repeated returns. In this, Lewis offers a profoundly realistic picture of the Christian life.

At one point in the middle of the letters, Screwtape is jubilant—convinced that the patient has finally been "reclaimed" for hell. The man has given in to temptation. He has grown spiritually numb, abandoned prayer, and lost interest in the things of God. His habits decay, his conscience dulls, and his imagination is shaped more by entertainment and ego than by eternity. For Screwtape, this is victory. But what he fails to anticipate is grace. Like many regressions in the real Christian life, this is not the end. The patient eventually awakens. He is pierced by conviction. Something deep and unseen stirs—perhaps through a sermon, a moment of silence, or a whispered prayer—and he turns again to Christ. Not with fanfare, but with humility.

Screwtape's growing frustration reveals something essential: the true test of faith is not found in spiritual highs or moments of clarity, but in what follows failure. The devil's great hope is not simply to make the believer fall, but to convince him he cannot rise again. He thrives on despair, self-condemnation, and spiritual paralysis. But grace operates on a different logic. As Proverbs says, "Though the righteous fall seven times, they rise again" (Prov 24:16). The believer's strength is not in sinlessness, but in their refusal to surrender. It is in their ability, by the Spirit, to fall into the arms of mercy rather than the pit of shame.

And the patient does rise. Over and over again. He does not impress Screwtape with brilliance, eloquence, or spiritual achievement. He terrifies him with resilience. He keeps turning. He keeps repenting. He keeps showing up—at church, in prayer, in confession. And in doing so, he becomes a living witness to the sustaining power of grace. His perseverance is not flashy, but it is faithful. It is the quiet, stubborn resolve of one who has been captured by Christ and will not let go—even when every earthly and spiritual force tempts him to walk away. And this, in the end, is what salvation looks like: not perfection, but persistence in grace.

TEMPTATION, TRIAL, AND THE SLOW WORK OF GOD

As the letters unfold, the patient's character quietly changes. He grows—not dramatically, but deeply. His transformation is not marked by spiritual spectacle, but by small, faithful acts of obedience. Early in the book, he is governed by emotional experience: if he feels close to God, he assumes he is doing well; if he feels distant, he believes something must be wrong. He mistakes spiritual dryness for failure. He is easily swayed by guilt, inflated by a sense of imagined humility, and discouraged by every faltering step. Like many young believers, he confuses feeling with faithfulness.

But in time, a shift begins. The patient slowly matures. He begins to obey not because it brings immediate reward, but because he has come to know it is right. He prays even when distracted. He resists temptation even when his heart doesn't feel strong. He returns to church even when it feels routine. He repents again, not because he feels especially penitent, but because he trusts that grace is greater than his sin. This kind of growth is subtle and often invisible to the one experiencing it—but from Screwtape's perspective, it is catastrophic. In Letter 8, Screwtape laments the divine strategy that allows believers to struggle, yet continue: "He wants them to learn to walk and must therefore take away His hand; and if only the will to walk is really there He is pleased even with their stumbles." Obedience in the dark is, for heaven, more precious than comfort in the light.

This is Lewis's reimagining of a deep spiritual tradition—echoing the psalms, the desert fathers, the Puritans, and the saints through the ages—that God sometimes withdraws the comfort of his felt presence not to punish, but to purify. As in Psalm 13, the cry "How long, O Lord?" is not met with immediate relief but with the slow formation of trust. The soul learns to walk, not by being carried at every moment, but by learning the balance of faith—placing one foot in front of the other, even in the valley of shadow. The Puritans called these seasons of divine silence "desertions," but they understood them as part of God's refining work.[1] The absence of emotion is not the absence of God. The silence is not abandonment; it is apprenticeship in trust.

The patient does not fully understand all of this. He doesn't have a framework for spiritual formation or a theology of suffering. But he doesn't need to. What matters is that he continues. His perseverance, though quiet and halting, begins to shape his soul. His obedience in weakness becomes stronger than his earlier zeal in confidence. He is being formed—not by comfort, but by covenant grace. This is the slow work of God: forming saints through trials, not in spite of them. And what hell most fears is not the believer who burns bright for a season, but the one who endures—stumbling forward in trust, anchored by the promises of God, and slowly becoming like Christ.

THE STRENGTH THAT LIES IN OBEDIENCE

One of the most striking developments in the patient's journey is his increasing ability to obey in the absence of comfort. At the beginning of the letters, obedience is mostly reactive: he responds to guilt after sin or to emotional highs that stir temporary zeal. His devotion rises and falls with his feelings. But as the spiritual battle unfolds, something more resilient begins to form. Obedience, once sporadic and sentimental, becomes a decision—a steady act of the will rooted not in how he feels but in what he knows. He prays when distracted. He resists temptation not because he feels strong, but because he believes God is worthy. He worships when it seems dry. He begins to live, as Paul describes, by "faith, not by

---

1. Joseph Symonds, *The Case and Cure of a Deserted Soul* (1639); Samuel Willard, *Spiritual Desertions Discovered and Remedied* (1699).

sight" (2 Cor 5:7). This is not flashy faith; it is durable faith. It is the kind that grows roots.

Screwtape is terrified by this. In what may be the most quoted and haunting line of the *Screwtape Letters*, he describes the moment of real danger: "Our cause is never more in danger than when a human, no longer desiring, but still intending to do our Enemy's will... looks round upon a universe from which every trace of Him seems to have vanished—and still obeys." This is a picture of spiritual maturity in its most refined form. The soul, stripped of support, deprived of comfort, surrounded by silence, chooses still to obey. That kind of obedience shakes the foundations of hell. It is not dependent on external circumstances or emotional reassurance. It is a defiant act of trust.

This is obedience forged in the furnace. It is not driven by the promise of reward, but by the reality of love. It is not buoyed by feeling, but anchored in truth. It is the obedience of Christ in Gethsemane—"Not my will, but yours be done" (Luke 22:42). It is the obedience of Job, who in the ashes declared, "Though he slay me, I will hope in him" (Job 13:15). It is the obedience of the martyrs, who died with songs on their lips and hope in their hearts. It is the obedience of the saints in every age who walk through the valley of the shadow and cling to the promises of God when all else has been stripped away. And it is this kind of obedience, Lewis suggests, that marks the soul as truly formed by grace.

What makes this obedience so powerful is that it is evidence of freedom. The devil thrives in manipulation, fear, impulse, and pride. But the Christian who obeys in the dark has learned to say yes to God without being prodded by reward or restrained by fear. He has learned what the enemy cannot counterfeit: trust that endures, love that persists, faith that walks even when the path disappears. This obedience is not perfection, but perseverance. It is not grand in appearance, but it is glorious in heaven's eyes. And in the end, this kind of obedience is not only the undoing of the devil's power—it is the triumph of God's grace in a human soul.

DISCIPLESHIP AND SPIRITUAL WARFARE

THE TRIUMPH OF GRACE IN DEATH

When the patient dies, Screwtape is undone. A lifetime of schemes—carefully laid temptations, well-timed distractions, whispered doubts—all amount to nothing. The war for the man's soul is lost, and it is lost not because the patient never failed, but because he was kept. Not because he stood tall, but because he fell into the arms of mercy. Not because he was worthy, but because he was Christ's. The entire demonic strategy has been thwarted by something hell cannot understand: the relentless grace of God.

Screwtape's final words are laced with bitter envy and impotent rage. He describes the man's sudden transition from the chaos of earthly life into the peace of eternity: "One moment it seemed to be all our world; the scream of bombs, the fall of houses... and then—silence and safety and the Enemy's country." It is a jarring and glorious reversal. What seems like defeat from a worldly perspective—violent death in a war-torn world—is, from the perspective of heaven, liberation. The man dies not in despair but in faith, and is welcomed not with condemnation but with delight. All that Screwtape built has crumbled in a single breath of glory.

This is Lewis's eschatology in miniature: death is not the defeat of the believer, but his final deliverance. The patient awakens not to emptiness, nor to judgment in isolation, but to joy. He sees angels. He hears music. He is overwhelmed not by fear, but by the radiance of the one whom he trusted in shadows and followed in weakness. He beholds Christ. And Screwtape, who has spent a lifetime trying to keep his patient from seeing clearly, cannot bear it. The clarity of heaven, the fullness of truth, the weight of glory—it is too much for hell to stomach. Because it confirms what they have always feared: that grace is stronger than deception, and love is stronger than death.

In that moment, the entire story comes into focus. The ups and downs, the victories and stumblings, the dry prayers and imperfect obedience—none of it was wasted. All of it is gathered up and redeemed. What seemed fragile and faltering was actually the quiet strength of the Spirit at work. The man has not only been saved—he has been sustained. He has been upheld, preserved, sanctified. This is the triumph of grace: not that the patient arrives unscathed, but that he arrives at all—safe, whole, and welcomed.

This is what Screwtape cannot understand, and what he most dreads. That God would take a fumbling, ordinary soul—full of contradictions and confessions—and bring him home with singing. That all of hell's efforts could not prevent a single saint from crossing the threshold into glory. And that the banner over that saint, tattered and torn by battle, still reads: Kept by grace. Beloved of Christ. Welcome home!

PASTORAL-THEOLOGICAL REFLECTION

One of Lewis's most profound insights is that the most formative moments in the Christian life often happen in spiritual darkness. This is where the patient grows most. Not when his faith feels easy, but when obedience costs something. When God seems silent. When prayers are dry. When temptations are strong. And yet—he still obeys. This is sanctification in the shadows. And it is where real perseverance is forged. Not in the heights of spiritual ecstasy, but in the trenches of daily faithfulness. In choosing to forgive again. In showing up to worship when we feel numb. In resisting bitterness, confessing sin, praying through tears. And every time we do, grace is at work.

The arc of the patient's journey in the *Screwtape Letters* presents one of Lewis's most profound theological affirmations: that the Christian life, though filled with temptation and turbulence, is upheld by an unshakable grace. It is a dramatization of what Reformed theology calls the perseverance of the saints—the promise that those whom God effectually calls will infallibly be brought to glory.

This doctrine, rooted in the unbreakable golden chain of Romans 8:30, assures believers that salvation is not a tentative contract, but an unchangeable covenant. "Those whom he justified he also glorified." Note the past tense: Paul speaks as if glorification were already accomplished, so secure is its fulfillment in God's eternal purpose.

Jesus expresses this security in personal terms in John 10:27–28: "My sheep hear my voice, and I know them… and they shall never perish." The force of his words lies in their absoluteness. The shepherd does not lose his sheep—not to wolves, not to wandering, not even to the sheep's own foolishness. Divine election is not undone by human weakness.

Yet this doctrine is frequently misunderstood. Some interpret it as implying a kind of spiritual inertia—as though believers may live as they please, confident that heaven awaits regardless. But perseverance is not spiritual fatalism. It is a dynamic, Spirit-empowered journey marked by struggle, repentance, and ongoing sanctification. The saints persevere because they are preserved. Jude 24 speaks of a God "who is able to keep you from stumbling." The verb "keep" is not passive—it means to guard, to watch, to protect. God is not indifferent to the trials of his children; he is actively involved in keeping them. The psalmist echoes this: "He will not let your foot be moved; he who keeps you will not slumber" (Ps 121:3).

The perseverance of the saints includes the possibility—indeed, the inevitability—of stumbles. But it excludes final apostasy. The elect may fall, but they cannot fall away. They may pass through seasons of doubt, dryness, and even sin, but the divine hand that began the work will complete it (Phil 1:6). God finishes what he starts.

This tension is vital. Scripture exhorts believers to "run the race" (Heb 12:1), "fight the good fight" (2 Tim 4:7), and "hold fast" (Rev 3:11). But these commands are undergirded by divine promises. The energy of the Christian life flows from the engine of God's preserving grace: "It is God who works in you, both to will and to work for his good pleasure" (Phil 2:13). Our striving is real, but our source is divine.

The early church fathers deeply understood the tension between divine preservation and human perseverance. Augustine emphasized that perseverance is ultimately a divine gift, declaring,

"He who falls, falls by his own will; and he who stands, stands by God's will."2 This reflects his conviction that while believers are called to remain steadfast, it is God's sustaining grace that enables them to endure. Augustine affirms the biblical truth that perseverance in the faith is not merely a matter of human striving, but a profound work of divine grace, one that both commands endurance and supplies the strength to endure, resting securely in God's unyielding faithfulness.

The Reformers intensified this clarity. Calvin insisted that perseverance is "not grounded in the strength of human will, but in the immutable purpose of God."3 God's election cannot be thwarted by the weakness of the believer because it is rooted in divine love and not human merit. The believer may feel forsaken, but the Spirit bears inward witness, drawing the heart back to Christ in repentance and faith. This is what Calvin called the inward testimony of the Spirit.

The doctrine of the perseverance of the saints is also deeply rooted in the confessional standards of the Reformed tradition. The *Westminster Confession of Faith* articulates this doctrine with clarity: "They, whom God hath accepted in His Beloved, effectually called and sanctified by His Spirit, can neither totally nor finally fall away from the state of grace, but shall certainly persevere therein to the end, and be eternally saved" (WCF 17.1). This perseverance is not grounded in human strength but in the immutable decree of God's election and the sustaining power of His Spirit.

Similarly, the *Canons of Dort* affirm that true believers are "kept by the power of God through faith unto salvation," and though they may fall into grievous sins, they are preserved from total apostasy.4 This understanding is not mere optimism but a theological conviction that salvation is secured not by the believer's grip on Christ, but by Christ's unbreakable hold on the believer. In Reformed thought, perseverance is seen as both a divine promise

---

2. Augustine, *On the Gift of Perseverance*, II.9.
3. Calvin, *Institutes*, 3.24.6.
4. *Canons of Dort*, Fifth Head of Doctrine, Article 3.

and a divine accomplishment, guaranteed by the covenantal faithfulness of God.

Lewis captures this mystery with masterful sensitivity. In the patient, we do not see a spiritual hero—we see a spiritual struggler. The patient is inconsistent. He doubts. He is distracted. He sins. And yet, he endures—not because he is resilient, but because he is loved. The great irony, as Screwtape perceives too late, is that each temptation resisted, each fall repented, each silent prayer uttered in fear is another evidence of the indwelling Spirit's work.

The Puritan Thomas Watson, in his *Body of Divinity*, put it simply: "Grace may be shaken with fears and doubts, but it cannot be plucked up by the roots."[5] This is not stoicism, but hope. The Christian is not preserved by grit, but by grace. He does not conquer by strength of will, but by the keeping power of God. Watson asserts that the perseverance of the saints is a guaranteed fruit of sanctification, grounded not in human strength but in God's sovereign grace. He distinguishes true believers from mere professors, noting that while hypocrites may fall away, those genuinely united to Christ are kept by divine power.

Watson emphasizes that believers are preserved through three primary means: the ordinances (prayer, Scripture, and sacraments), the continual inward work of the Holy Spirit, and Christ's intercession. He describes the Spirit as continually nourishing the believer's faith, much like fresh oil keeps a lamp burning, and he points to Christ's prayer for Peter as evidence of divine preservation (Luke 22:32). Watson further argues that perseverance is rooted in God's unbreakable promises, his eternal election, and the believer's union with Christ—just as a body cannot be severed from its head. Christ's redemptive work guarantees that none of his people will be lost, affirming that perseverance is not just a possibility, but a certainty secured by God's unchanging faithfulness.

Perseverance also corrects any performance-based view of sanctification. The believer's assurance does not lie in spiritual success or subjective feelings, but in the objectivity of Christ's finished work. As the *Canons of Dort* remind us, "God is faithful, who…

---

5. Watson, *A Body of Divinity*, 285.

mercifully confirms and powerfully preserves [the elect] therein even to the end."6 The evidence of this preservation is not perfection—but persistent returning. The believer always comes back. And even that return is grace.

The story of the patient [the Christian] in the *Screwtape Letters* is not a spiritual success story—it is a gospel story. It is the story of a life marked by fits and starts, by fear and failure, and yet sealed by sovereign grace. It is the story of every Christian who has ever wandered and been welcomed back. Every saint who has ever wept in secret but still returned to the Lord's Table. Every disciple who has stumbled but not been lost. The comfort of the gospel is not that we always hold fast, but that we are always held. Screwtape fails because grace does not. He rages because the soul he pursued has been purchased. He loses because the shepherd never does.

Lewis's vision is pastoral genius. He does not romanticize the Christian life. He exposes its complexity, its daily tensions, its emotional unpredictability. But he threads through it all a scarlet cord of assurance: God is faithful. He who calls you is faithful; he will surely do it (1 Thess 5:24). In Screwtape's eyes, the patient's perseverance is a catastrophe. Not because he was faultless—but because he kept returning. Not because he conquered sin—but because he clung to Christ. Not because he earned heaven—but because heaven had marked him with mercy. And this is the wonder of perseverance. It turns failure into formation. It redeems every tear. It transforms even death into a doorway. For nothing—not sin, not suffering, not Satan himself—can separate us from the love of God in Christ Jesus our Lord (Rom 8:38–39).

So keep walking. Not because you always feel strong, but because Christ is strong for you. Do not measure your faith by your emotional highs or spiritual accomplishments. Measure it by your return—again and again—to the one who holds you fast. If your prayers feel weak, pray them anyway. If worship feels dry, sing anyway. If obedience feels costly, obey anyway. The perseverance of the saints is not about flawless performance—it is about faithful returning. It is not the story of the perfect, but of the preserved.

6. *Canons of Dort*, Fifth Head of Doctrine, Article 3.

Your continued faith, even when it flickers, is evidence of God's sustaining grace.

Commit yourself afresh—not to perfection, but to perseverance. Lean into the ordinary means of grace: Scripture, prayer, the sacraments, the fellowship of the church. These are not rituals to check off; they are lifelines, channels of divine strength for weary saints. Fight the lie that your spiritual value is measured by your energy or clarity. The Christian life is not about always feeling the fire—it's about staying near the flame. And when you stumble, do not despair. Return. Repent. Receive grace. Because the comfort of the gospel is not that we never fall, but that God never lets us go.

So the Christian keeps walking. Sometimes limping. Sometimes crawling. But always walking toward the one who holds him. And that walk, however faltering, is itself a declaration of victory.

Let the devils rage.

We are held.

Chapter 12

Conclusion: Discipleship in the Fog of War

WE ARE AT WAR. Not a war of flesh and blood, not a war of earthly kingdoms, but a spiritual war for the soul—a war for truth, attention, affection, and allegiance. This war is not announced with sirens or reported on breaking news, yet it rages in every church pew, every distracted heart, every disordered love. And it is precisely in this invisible, ordinary, and relentless conflict that discipleship takes place.

Lewis, in writing the *Screwtape Letters*, removed the veil for us. He did not give us a theological textbook or a battlefield map, but a mirror—an imaginative reflection of our ordinary lives as the ground zero of spiritual warfare. Through Screwtape's malevolent advice, Lewis shows us the strategies of hell so that we might more clearly recognize the grace of heaven. He did not write to frighten, but to fortify. He wrote not for entertainment, but for equipping. His concern, like the apostle Paul's, was that Christians "would not be outwitted by Satan," but would instead "be aware of his schemes" (2 Cor 2:11).

And so we have walked through these chapters together, each chapter exposing a facet of this war—and each offering a way forward through the gospel of grace. Lewis reminds us that the battlefield is not somewhere out there, in dramatic showdowns or cultural controversies. The battlefield is here: in the mind, the habits, the church, the suffering, the quiet moments of prayer. Discipleship is not a retreat from the front lines. It is life on the front lines.

A REVIEW OF THE BATTLEFRONT

We began by acknowledging the banality of temptation—how sin rarely appears monstrous, but subtle. Screwtape's greatest advantage is not horror, but the ordinary: procrastination, comfort, convenience. The gentle slope is more dangerous than the steep cliff because it feels safer. The enemy's most effective tactic is spiritual drift—small compromises, dulled affections, days without prayer. In response, discipleship must be alert, not passive. It requires watchfulness, vigilance, and honesty about the spiritual cost of complacency.

We explored how distraction functions as a weapon in the digital age. The enemy does not have to destroy your faith if he can keep you scrolling, rushing, reacting, and numbed. When attention is fragmented, formation becomes impossible. In such an age, stillness becomes resistance. Solitude becomes strength. Attention becomes an act of worship. Discipleship must train the mind to see clearly and the heart to stay focused on Christ amid a thousand competing voices.

Then we turned to the affections, recognizing that we are shaped not just by what we think, but by what we love. The enemy deforms our loves; Christ reforms them. Discipleship is not merely information—it is reformation of the heart. It is the slow, deliberate process of loving what God loves, desiring what God desires, and being remade by the Spirit into people who live out of holy desire, not hollow duty.

We saw that prayer is not only communion, but combat. Screwtape's greatest fear is the believer who prays honestly and persistently—especially when the heavens are silent. Prayer is not performance. It is perseverance. It is the lifeline of grace, the posture of dependence, and the front line of spiritual warfare. To be

Conclusion: Discipleship in the Fog of War

a disciple is to learn to pray in the fog—not when it feels easy, but when it feels necessary.

We entered the church as a battleground, not because it is failing, but because it is central to God's plan for forming his people. Screwtape wants us to see only its flaws: its hypocrisy, eccentricity, awkwardness. But Christ calls us to see his body. Spiritual growth happens in the context of community, not comfort. Christian discipleship demands commitment to the messy, beautiful, frustrating, and glorious life of the local church. There is no formation without fellowship, no maturity without membership.

We faced the furnace of suffering, which Screwtape attempts to exploit but which God redeems. Lewis and Scripture both testify that God does not waste pain. It is not a sign of God's absence, but often the very evidence of his refining presence. Christian discipleship learns to embrace sanctification in the valley as much as on the mountain—to see suffering not as detour, but as pathway.

Then we wrestled with pride, the sin behind all sins. The enemy loves to turn virtue into vice, especially when we take credit for our growth. The disciple must learn the way of downward glory—the humility of Christ, the freedom of self-forgetfulness, the joy of hidden faithfulness. Spiritual pride is the great counterfeit of holiness; humility is the great safeguard of the soul.

We examined the battle between God's kingdom and the world. Screwtape seeks to replace gospel allegiance with political idolatry and cultural tribalism. Christian discipleship reclaims the Christian mind—rooted in Scripture, shaped by the cross, oriented to the eternal kingdom of Christ, and immune to the lies of ideological captivity. It resists the temptation to baptize worldly loyalties in religious language and instead declares, "Jesus is Lord"—over every nation, every cause, every claim.

Finally, we traced the Christian journey—a life marked not by spectacular spiritual highs, but by quiet perseverance. The patient's story in Lewis's book reminds us that Christian discipleship is not about never falling, but always rising again in grace. It is about praying when distracted, trusting when confused, obeying when weary. The battle is not won by the strong, but by the kept. Not by those who never sin, but by those who never stop returning.

THE VICTORY OF ORDINARY SAINTS

In the end, the patient dies—and in that moment, Screwtape is silenced. The long war concludes not with fanfare, but with faithfulness. The man who stumbled, who doubted, who drifted and returned, is welcomed into the Enemy's country; that is, into the presence of the Lord God Almighty. The triumph of his life was not brilliance, boldness, or public success. It was quiet, often hidden perseverance under grace. This is the real goal of Christian discipleship: to become resilient, radiant, and rooted in Christ until the very end.

The *Screwtape Letters* is a strange kind of spiritual manual. It does not give us a step-by-step guide to holiness. It offers something better: an imaginative reminder of how the enemy works and of how God wins. It is a call to alertness, to watchfulness, and above all, to grace. It reminds us that the Christian life is not about impressing heaven, but about being faithful in the fog.

So, take heart. If you feel spiritually weary, if your prayers feel dry, if your affections are dull, if your obedience feels costly—you are not failing. You are fighting. And the one who called you is faithful. He will keep you to the end.

A CALL TO THE PRESENT-DAY CHURCH

What does all of this mean for the church today?

It means we must wake up. It means we must stop treating discipleship as a side project, a luxury for the spiritually mature, or a secondary ministry among many. It is not optional. It is not seasonal. It is not reserved for pastors or professionals. It is the very essence of the church's calling. Jesus did not commission us to build crowds or manage programs—he commissioned us to "make disciples" (Matt 28:19). And if we are not actively, intentionally,

Conclusion: Discipleship in the Fog of War

and sacrificially forming disciples of Jesus Christ, then we are passively allowing the world to form them in its image. And the world is not neutral. It is not patient. It is not sitting quietly waiting for the church to speak. It is already speaking—shouting, even—through every glowing screen, every commercial slogan, every school curriculum, every political broadcast, every platform algorithm, and every false gospel of self.

Our phones catechize more consistently than most pulpits. Our calendars form us more than our creeds. Our media choices shape our affections more profoundly than our music or our mission statements. The war for the heart and mind is not theoretical. It is not coming. It is here. It is happening—in the home, in the hallway, in the earbuds of our teenagers, in the scrolling fingers of the anxious, in the Netflix queues of the weary, in the silence we fill with endless noise instead of God. The devil no longer needs to roar. All he needs is to distract. If he cannot have our souls, he will gladly take our attention, our affections, our imaginations, our endurance.

And so the church must respond. Not with panic. Not with nostalgia for a world that no longer exists. Not with mimicry of a culture that cannot save. But with theological clarity, spiritual depth, and unshakable, relentless faithfulness. Our methods must change where needed, but our message must remain unchanged. In a world of speed, we need sacred slowness. In an age of outrage, we need a quiet and settled joy. In a culture of self, we need the crucified Christ.

We must recover a vision of discipleship that is not shallow, hurried, or reactive—but deep, slow, formative, and profoundly countercultural. A vision that understands that the Christian life is not a brand, but a way. Not a sprint, but a pilgrimage. Not a curated platform, but a daily cross. That holiness is not a product to consume, but a life to be cultivated in ordinary faithfulness. That faithfulness in obscurity—caring for aging parents, loving difficult neighbors, repenting in prayer, showing up every Sunday—is more spiritually weighty than applause on a stage. We must raise up saints who can live low and love long.

Discipleship and Spiritual Warfare

We must stop measuring success by the size of our buildings or the cleverness of our branding. The metrics of God's kingdom are different. Jesus did not promise that the church would be large. He promised that the gates of hell would not prevail against it (Matt 16:18). We must begin to measure our churches by the fruit of the Spirit: love, joy, peace, patience, kindness, goodness, faithfulness, gentleness, and self-control.

Discipleship is not a product to sell. It is not a sermon series to consume. It is not a four-week program to check off a list. It is a lifelong surrender to Jesus—shaped by the gathered worship of the church, guided by the authority of Scripture, sustained by a life of prayer, and lived out in ordinary, covenantal community. It is not glamorous, but it is glorious. It is not fast, but it is fruitful. And it is the only way the church will survive—and thrive—in this present age.

If we do not teach our people how to live in Christ, the culture will teach them how to live without him. If we do not form affections for heaven, the world will stir appetites for hell. If we do not raise up disciples who can pray in the dark, think with theological clarity, resist temptation, love sacrificially, and endure faithfully—then Screwtape doesn't need to lift a claw. Our drift will do his work for him.

But we are not without hope. Christ is risen. The tomb is empty. The Spirit is still at work in the church. God's word still speaks life in a world of lies. The church still stands—not because of our strength, but because of his promise. And the devil still loses.

So let us take up the armor of God (Eph 6:10–18). Let us train one another to pray with reverence and resilience. Let us renew our minds by the word of truth and guard our hearts from every subtle lie. Let us teach our children to sing truth louder than the culture's noise. Let us form resilient saints who live quietly, love deeply, serve joyfully, repent regularly, and press on—no matter the cost. This is the call of the church in our generation. Not to be liked, but to be light. Not to be relevant, but to be rooted. Not to be impressive, but to be faithful.

Conclusion: Discipleship in the Fog of War

This is the essence of Christian discipleship in a world at war. It is not glamorous. It is not loud. It is rarely noticed. But it is real. And it is necessary. To follow Christ is to resist the pull of the world, the schemes of the enemy, and the desires of the flesh. It is to pray when it's hard, to repent when it's humbling, to believe when it's costly, to love when it's inconvenient, and to persevere when everything in us wants to quit. That kind of faith does not rise from within. It comes from above. It is sustained by the Spirit. It is anchored in truth. And it is cultivated in community.

So, to the tired, the weary, the distracted, the doubting: take heart. You are not alone. You are not beyond reach. You are not too far gone. If you are still walking, still praying, still longing to be faithful—even if feebly—then you are in the fight. And more importantly, you are being kept.

Keep reading the word, even when it feels dry.

Keep praying, even when you don't know what to say.

Keep gathering with the church, even when it feels awkward.

Keep confessing your sins, even when it feels repetitive.

Keep resisting temptation, even when it feels impossible.

Keep hoping in Christ, even when your heart aches.

Because the goal is not to be impressive. The goal is to be preserved. And you are. One day, when all of this fog has lifted, when the whispers of Screwtape are silenced forever, when the tears are wiped away and the scars are healed, we will stand—like the patient did—not in triumph of our own, but in the victory of Another. And we will hear those words that make every battle worth it: "Well done, good and faithful servant. Enter into the joy of your Master."

Until then, press on.

The saints always do.

Bibliography

Anselm of Canterbury. *Proslogion*. Indianapolis: Hackett, 2001.
Aquinas, Thomas. *Summa Theologiae*, II–II, Q.35, Art. 1.
Arendt, Hannah. *Eichmann in Jerusalem: A Report on the Banality of Evil*. New York: Viking, 1963.
Augustine. *The City of God*. London: Penguin, 1972.
———. *Confessions*. London: Penguin, 1961.
———. *On Christian Doctrine*. Indianapolis: Bobbs-Merrill, 1958.
———. *On the Gift of Perseverance*. In *The Works of Saint Augustine*, vol. 1.23. Hyde Park, NY: New City, 2002.
———. *Sermons on Selected Lessons of the New Testament*. In *Nicene and Post-Nicene Fathers*, First Series, vol. 6. Edited by Philip Schaff. Grand Rapids: Eerdmans, 1980.
Bavinck, Herman. *Reformed Dogmatics*. Vol. 3. Grand Rapids: Baker Academic, 2006.
Baxter, Richard. *The Saints' Everlasting Rest*. Philadelphia: Presbyterian Board of Publication, 1847.
Bonhoeffer, Dietrich. *Letters and Papers from Prison*. New York: Touchstone, 1997.
———. *Life Together: The Classic Exploration of Christian Community*. Francisco: Harper & Row, 1954.
Calvin, John. *Commentary on the Psalms*. Grand Rapids: Eerdmans, 1949.
———. *Institutes of the Christian Religion*. Peabody, MA: Hendrickson, 2008.
Cassian, John. *The Institutes*. New York: Newman, 2000.
Climacus, John. *The Ladder of Divine Ascent*. Mahwah, NJ: Paulist, 1982.
Edwards, Jonathan. *Religious Affections*. In *The Works of Jonathan Edwards*, vol. 1. Edinburgh: Banner of Truth, 1986.
Evagrius Ponticus. *The Praktikos and Chapters on Prayer*. Kalamazoo, MI: Cistercian, 1972.
Gregory of Nazianzus. *Letters*, 101. In *Nicene and Post-Nicene Fathers*, Second Series, vol. 7. Peabody, MA: Hendrickson, 1994.
Gregory of Nyssa. *The Life of Moses*. Mahwah, NJ: Paulist, 1978.
Gregory the Great. *Moralia in Job*. Oxford: John Henry Parker, 1844.

BIBLIOGRAPHY

Ignatius of Antioch. *Letter to the Romans*. In *The Apostolic Fathers*, vol. 1. Cambridge: Harvard University Press, 2003.

Lewis, C. S. *Mere Christianity*. New York: HarperOne, 2001.

———. *The Problem of Pain*. New York: HarperOne, 2001.

———. *Reflections on the Psalms*. New York: Harcourt Brace, 1958.

———. *The Screwtape Letters*. New York: HarperOne, 2001.

Luther, Martin. *Large Catechism*. In *The Book of Concord*. Minneapolis: Fortress, 2000.

———. "The Ninety-Five Theses." In *Luther's Works*, vol. 31. Philadelphia: Fortress, 1957.

Newbigin, Lesslie. *Foolishness to the Greeks: The Gospel and Western Culture*. Grand Rapids: Eerdmans, 1986.

Origen. *On Prayer*. Mahwah, NJ: Paulist, 1979.

Owen, John. *The Mortification of Sin*. Wheaton, IL: Crossway, 2006.

Postman, Neil. *Amusing Ourselves to Death: Public Discourse in the Age of Show Business*. New York: Penguin, 1986.

Sibbes, Richard. "The Tender Heart." In *The Works of Richard Sibbes*, vol. 7. Edinburgh: Banner of Truth, 1862–64.

Silva, Thiago. *Discipleship in a Post-Christian Age: With a Little Help from C. S. Lewis*. Eugene, OR: Wipf & Stock, 2025.

Tertullian. *Apology and De Oratione*. In *Ante-Nicene Fathers*, vol. 3. Peabody, MA: Hendrickson, 2004.

Watson, Thomas. *A Body of Divinity*. Edinburgh: Banner of Truth, 1958.

www.ingramcontent.com/pod-product-compliance
Lightning Source LLC
Chambersburg PA
CBHW071441160426
43195CB00013B/1996